HOODOO FOR WAR AND PEACE

WORKING MAGIC SPELLS FOR JUSTICE AND
PROTECTION

ANGELIE BELARD

HENTOPAN
PUBLISHING

CONTENTS

INTRODUCTION

"Hoodoo is a curse." "It is unnatural." "It is people tapping into things they don't understand in order to play God." "It is a manipulation of the natural order of things." These are a few of the phrases I have heard people use to describe Hoodoo over the years. Interestingly, almost no one with this perspective has ever practiced Hoodoo. I, on the other hand, have been a practitioner of Hoodoo for decades and this is not how I perceive it, either in my own life or in the lives of those I have encountered over the years.

When I wrote my first book on Hoodoo, it was born out of a sense of urgency. I had a burning need to pass down the knowledge that had been passed on to me by my grandmother, who'd learned it from her mother and so on, back through generations. While I still have this desire, this third book in the Hoodoo series is born out of gratitude.

The title, though you might find it somewhat misleading, comes from a place of reflection. When I look back at my life, I have much to be grateful for. For starters, I am rich, though I am not referring only to financial wealth or social success. I am talking about the life I have lived and the wealth of experiences I have curated over time. Hoodoo has been an integral part of these experiences.

I wasn't always a Hoodoo practitioner, but as far as I can remember, Hoodoo has always been present in my life in some form. My mother hung mojo bags in specific places around the house to ward off evil spirits. I was given small spell packets to carry around with me for protection. And if I had bad dreams that included certain things, I was given a cleanse at midnight in the woods near our home. To others, this probably sounds strange. But for my family, it was simply the way we lived, thanks in large part to my roots.

My grandmother was well known for her Hoodoo skills. Her conjurings saved marriages, established businesses, and helped to create a community that thrived, both mentally and emotionally. But she wasn't all sugar and rainbows. She could do a mean crossing as well. People often make the mistake of believing that Hoodoo is mainly used for love, wealth, or health purposes. But life is about more than love, money, or health.

My grandmother used to say that even the sweetest and mildest dog will bare its fangs if pushed into a corner. There are dark times in life. In those times, you may be forced to bare your fangs, and the fangs that nature gave you might not be enough to keep the wolves at bay. During such times, a little help from beyond is exactly what we need. My grandmother helped people get the help they needed in such times.

In my early 20s, I became a full-time hoodoo practitioner. I took over from my grandmother in preparing conjures for people who came to us for help. One of the more popular requests had to do with curses... or crossings. A curse is a terrible choice of words used to describe what rootwork is. If you have read any of my books, you know by now that Hoodoo is neither inherently good nor bad. The outcome and your level of satisfaction with it are what makes it good or bad. However, curses have a way of hitting the intended targets with the full force of your will and intention. For people who like to discuss ethics, this may be the area where they draw the line.

But before you jump to conclusions, let me tell you about a client who I worked with to perfect a crossing for her ex. Before she came to me, she was in a long-term relationship that was very abusive. Thankfully, she was one of the lucky few who got out with her dignity intact. Unfortunately, her ex refused to let go. He didn't approve of her leaving or even living, so he became a threat to her life. He harassed and hounded her at work, at home, and at every opportunity he could find. When she came to me, she was a wreck. She felt as if she was losing her mind. As if that wasn't bad enough, her family, who were supposed to be her primary support unit, were opposed to her leaving the relationship. They pressured her to reconsider her decisions and treated her terribly for standing her ground. Basically, she was being hit from within and also from all around her. She was mentally unstable, emotionally traumatized, and had no physical support whatsoever to help her find her bearings.

To fix things, we had to remove the one element that was at the center of the whole crisis, which was the offending ex. I used the hot foot powder (a personal favorite) to make life a living hell (literally a burning-up) for him every time he came within a few feet of her or members of her family. Within weeks he dropped his obsession over her and moved out of town. The next step was to mend the broken relationship she had with her family. We did that with a healing conjure. Finally, the last piece of the puzzle was to help her find inner strength and courage to move past her trauma. This is typically what a conjure looks like that's designed to protect your peace and wage war against those who want to take that peace away from you.

Beyond this anecdote, this book is dedicated to explaining what Hoodoo is for those who have never tried it out and also to re-educating those already familiar with the core pillars that guide our practices. Building the life you desire using a little spiritual help from the practice of Hoodoo is not limited to boosting your wealth or attracting love into your life. That is what this book will show you. Many of my clients also want to protect the life they already have and I can teach you how to do the same. We fight with enemies both seen and unseen. And sometimes, no amount of love or money can rid us of that enemy. But with the right conjure using roots and herbs, you can ensure that everything you have worked hard to build is protected and that you are able to reap the rewards of your labor. We all deserve to enjoy in peace what we've worked hard to achieve.

The knowledge I share with you here is not meant to show you the dark side of Hoodoo.

In fact, there is no dark side. Instead, it is intended to help you realize that you have everything you need to take the life you are living and make it your own. Through your intentions and help from your ancestors, you can manifest the life you want and ensure that you come out on top no matter how bad the situation becomes. Your intention is key, though, so in the next chapter I will elaborate on all of this.

For now, I want you to know that you are not alone. That you are capable and you are strong. Everything I share with you is knowledge that has been passed down to me through generations. I hope it brings you peace and it helps you find your path on this crazy journey called life. I hope this becomes a turning point for you, where you can look back decades from now and proclaim, "Yes, I am rich. Not just in wealth and love but in experiences that helped me be the person I am today." Now, let us begin.

1

***

While it is tempting to immediately delve into spells, conjures and all the other fun stuff you're waiting for, the foundation for that kind of power is knowledge and understanding. Without this knowledge, you only focus on what you want and, more often than not, that method leads to a dead end. When you know what you are doing, you equip yourself with the necessary tools needed to ensure the success of conjures. I became a full-fledged Hoodoo practitioner in my early twenties but I started my education long before that, without even realizing that I was being trained for the role I will take up later in life.

My mother, father, and most especially, my grandmother, taught me what Hoodoo truly is. If you consult the internet, you'll see a lot of dark images and dark thoughts associated with Hoodoo and will also find a lot of information that doesn't add up. So even when you're given a formula for a spell, you're not able to complete it. This is because your foundation is not right. This is why I begin every book I write with the proper foundational knowledge.

Don't worry, we won't delve too deep. I simply want to make sure you understand key aspects that will make a difference in the success or failure of the conjures you learn. In this chapter, we will learn what Hoodoo is, where it comes from and why we practice it. I will also touch on some of the general misconceptions people might have about Hoodoo. Keep an open mind as you learn. Be patient as you go through this chapter. Patience is a key ingredient in any Hoodoo conjure.

Think of your journey to the end of this chapter as a good starting point for a lesson in patience. Before we begin, I want you to pretend you don't know anything. Let go of any preconceived notions or prior research you may have done on this subject. Forget the pressing need that brought you here. Make your mind a blank slate so you are not fighting the information I share with you. Instead, sit back and allow your curiosity to lead you to explore beyond the confines of what you think you know.

THE HISTORY OF HOODOO

The story of Hoodoo cannot be told without talking about the many slaves who were forcefully taken away from their homes in Africa and forced to work on farms for their masters in a new country. Their strength wasn't the only thing demanded of them. They were made to learn the ways of their masters; the way they talked, the way they dressed, and the things they believed in were imposed upon these slaves. In a strange land surrounded by cruelty and hatred, they had to learn a new language, and believe in a new god. On top of this, they had to do everything they could to survive the hardships that plagued their daily existence. But these resilient people did more than just survive. They created a community for themselves. They didn't leave their motherland behind - not completely. They embraced the new faith and merged it with knowledge from their mother-land. Then they acclimatized this new thing they had created to the land that had now become their home, and that is how Hoodoo was born.

The whips of their masters became the sword through which these slaves earned their freedom. The faith passed to them became the anchor that linked them to their identity as they practiced Hoodoo. The strange plants and leaves in this new land in which they found themselves became the channel through which they accessed healing, love, wealth, and protection for their community. Hoodoo was never about faith. These people already had that in Christianity. It was never about where they had come from. This was a new life and they learned to make something new for themselves in it. It was about honoring the journey that led them to that point. It was about acknowledging the people who had started this journey long before they did. It was about ensuring that they maintain a connection to their ancestors.

Hoodoo is a way of life. It is what we do when we wake up in the morning, the thoughts we nurture, and the intentions we carry around with us as we perform our daily tasks. Hoodoo is about access. As we continue through this chapter, as well as the rest of the book, you will understand what I mean. For now, know that Hoodoo is not the dark magic that Hollywood or non-practitioners would have you believe it is.

RELATIONSHIP TO VOODOO

One of the first things to know is that Hoodoo and voodoo don't have much in common beyond the rhyming of their names. For starters, Hoodoo is simply a way of life, while Voodoo is a religion practiced predominantly in the western part of Africa, although its presence here in America is pretty strong too. People often think Hoodoo is the African American version of Voodoo. While there are shared principles between the two practices, in truth they are more like distant cousins. For example, both seek help with the use of roots and herbs. There is also a shared belief in using our link to our ancestors as a conduit for the power that we call upon whenever we perform a conjure. But that is as far the similarities between Hoodoo and Voodoo go.

To practice Voodoo, you need to be initiated. To practice Hoodoo, you simply need to know the right recipe or formula for a spell and put your intentions to work. Voodoo is a religion while Hoodoo is not. Voodoo practices require paying homage to not just your ancestors but to specific deities associated with the voodoo faith. Hoodoo, on the other hand, while predominantly practiced by Christians, does not require any form of tributes to be paid to a specific deity. You can freely practice whatever faith you identify with and still practice Hoodoo. The only requirement, which is more of a suggestion rather than being mandatory, is to occasionally put offerings on your altar to appease the spirits and ancestors who help you with the conjures you make. This brings me to the next point.

USE OF THE BIBLE

My grandma Estelle was a devout Christian. She never missed a church service and she always bundled me up and took me with her even when I didn't feel like going. For her, faith was not something you ever compromised. Although I didn't understand what I considered at the time to be her obsession with church activities, I gradually developed a personal relationship with God, and this has been a strong force in determining how I express myself as a Hoodoo practitioner. I feel more powerful when I use Bible quotes in executing a spell. Some of my favorite scriptures for conjures are subconscious ways for me to connect with my grandmother whenever I perform those workings. But for some people, it goes even deeper than that.

The words contained in the Bible are important to every Christian. For those Hoodoo practitioners who also happen to be Christians, using quotes from the Bible helps them identify the practice with their faith. But it's less about religious than it is about firing up their intentions. As mentioned earlier, intention plays a very important role when it comes to creating a successful conjure. You can have the best ingredients assembled to put a spell together but if your intentions lack charge or energy, it will not be enough to power up the spell. The scripture for many Hoodoo practitioners provides conviction, and conviction empowers intention. This is the main reason many use the Bible when they practice Hoodoo. For non-Christians, however, using the Bible to activate a conjure might not be effective, since the conviction is not there.

The key thing to remember is that Hoodoo was created and then adapted, meaning it is not fixed or rooted in a specific religion. The first people who started working with Hoodoo created something that harmonized the things that were important to them; the Bible, their traditions, and their way of life. But you can be a Buddhist and even an atheist and your belief will not automatically cut you off from benefiting from the practice of Hoodoo. Hoodoo is for everyone, regardless of their gender, faith, or skin color. The foundation of Hoodoo was intended to help people who felt marginalized and helpless. As I mentioned earlier, Hoodoo is about access. If you need to access the powers that lie beyond the world of our physical senses, you are welcome.

Using faith to obtain that access is way down on the list when it comes to the tools that can help make your conjures more powerful.

ANCESTRAL ALTAR

The ancestral altar is sacred for everyone who practices or intends to practice Hoodoo. It is a space dedicated to communing with your ancestors. While it is possible to carry out this communication anywhere, having a dedicated space creates a concentration of power that can now be diverted into whatever conjure you are working on. An ancestral altar, as the name implies, is an altar that links you to your ancestor(s). You create that link by placing on it an object of value that belonged to someone in your lineage. The closer you were to this person, the stronger the bond or power will be. The more objects of value you have on this altar, the more beneficial it is. In addition to the objects of value belonging to the ancestor(s) you want to connect with, you can attract their spirit with offerings based on the things they liked, such as their favorite drink or favorite sweets.

Your ancestral altar doesn't have to be a large space. A small table will do. It is not something you should be ashamed of, so hiding it away in a closet is not necessary. I am not suggesting you be blatant about it, but it is something that identifies you with your roots, so be proud of showing off where you come from. If you are more of a private person, however, it is okay to put it somewhere that people do not readily have access to. You don't want someone to tamper with your conjures and spells. We don't always know everyone we let into our homes or what their intentions might be, so keeping your altar on display but not easily accessible might be the best option.

For me, one of the things I am most proud of is our ancestral bible, which sits proudly on display on my ancestral altar. Unlike the conventional Christian Bible that focuses on the words of God, this is a genealogy of my family tree that dates back over 100 years. I like to look back at where I come from and this inspires pride in me. something I believe I share with my ancestors. You might want to find an object like this that you identify with but that you also share as a link to your ancestors.

Apart from the link to your past, having a glass of water at your altar is also a good idea. Think of this as a spiritual alarm that lets you know if your spell is working or not. When you perform a spell and notice bubbles on the surface of the water in the glass, it could be an indication that a malicious spirit might have interfered with the working of your spell. And water evaporating faster than normal could be an indication that your spell is proceeding as planned. Candles are also beneficial to have on your altar, as they provide illumination for your conjure. If you have your ancestral link, some type of offering, a glass of water, and some candles, you are good to go.

SPIRITUAL CLEANSING

Our bodies carry around energies and auras that can some-times put us in a bubble that manipulates experiences we have without us realizing it. These auras or energies can repel good things from coming into our lives or attract the wrong kind of things. And it is not just our bodies that influ-ence the experiences we have in life. The spaces we live in also have this ability. This is why in Hoodoo, a cleanse is often carried out to enhance the effectiveness of whatever conjure we are trying to work. Cleanses serve different purposes in Hoodoo. Some of them are designed to purify you physically, emotionally, and mentally. The same purifi-cation rite can be carried out on the spaces we live in or on objects that serve a special purpose for us. For example, if you are going to perform a spell that involves love-making with your spouse or significant other, carrying out a cleanse on the bed where the event is going to occur can make the love-making ritual even more successful.

Cleanses can also be done for protection. If you suspect that you (or your loved ones) are in danger, a protection cleanse can place invisible and impenetrable barriers around your body so that even when someone casts an evil eye or spell on you, it won't work. The same thing applies to your home or business environments. Speaking of business, there are also cleanses you can perform to attract more customers to your business. Then there are cleanses that act as openers for the conjures you are creating. These cleanses ensure that the intentions coming from your mind and the energy put into the conjures are in sync. This is very important for attracting the right kind of spirit to help you. For most of the spells I will share with you here, a cleanse must be performed beforehand. This will remove any negative aura or energy that might tamper with the conjure you make. Here is a simple but effective cleanse.

The Door Opener

This cleanse is to help you create a door that opens up your spiritual senses and allows you to be more receptive to the gifts that your ancestors offer you. It opens up the portal that allows these gifts to flow to you. It thoroughly cleanses your aura and energy and prepares you for whatever conjure you are about to work on. Carry out this cleanse right before you perform the spells I share with you in this book.

The key ingredient in this spell is mint. Mint is a plant you can easily get from your garden or grocery store. In Hoodoo, it opens paths that are blocked and cleanses your mind and spirit. It is perfect for soothing a mind that is troubled by doubts, fears, and anxiety. Mint can also be used to attract success, aid communication, and help with healing... all of which are necessary for any conjure to work.

You Will Need

- Fresh mint
- Rosemary

- Cloves
- Large pot

The Work

1. Put all the ingredients in a large pot of water and boil it
2. When it boils, add the mix into your bathwater and adjust until the temperature is right. The more steam, the better.
3. Soak in the water for a few minutes. Allow the mixture of scents to envelop you.
4. Step out of the tub and air dry. Proceed with your normal activities, but avoid mirrors until you have completed the conjure you have in mind.

Before draining the tub, scoop out of the water the leaves and anything else that might clog the drain. Wrap the leaves in foil and toss them in the trash or dispose of them in a flowing creek or body of water. This conjure, though simple, can also lift curses.

I had a client who was cursed with a skin disease by a woman who considered her a rival. One day she woke up itchy and this soon turned into sores and blisters. She was put on medication for skin allergies, which is what it looked like on the surface, but none of the medications worked. The odor from the blisters accompanied by her dark dreams were indications that this was a curse. She needed to sort this out spiritually before the medications would be effective. We performed this cleanse once and I asked her to resume her medications. Within two days, the blisters began drying up.

UNDERSTANDING THE POWER OF ROOTS AND HERBS

Roots and herbs are very important tools in preparing a conjure in Hoodoo. Traditionally, spells or conjures are referred to as rootwork because we work with plants to help create the kind of results we want to manifest in our lives. A deep understanding of herbs and what they represent plays a crucial role in putting these sacred tools together to work. In Hoodoo, we believe that our world was created by a supreme being who left their essence on earth. The plants around us embody this energy, and the earth, which is directly linked to the plants by their roots, also has this imprint.

Most plants have masculine or feminine energy, though some are neutral, and these are the ones more commonly used in general spells. This detail is important because when you cast a spell you have to factor in the gender of the target as well as your own gender as the spellcaster. The energy you put into the spell should be able to bind well and help you find your target. The energy of a plant is especially important in conjures that have to do with love and romance. They also are required in spells that are intended to manipulate the will of another person.

Plants are divided into various parts: the flowers, the fruits, the stem, the leaves, and the roots. No part of a plant is wasted in Hoodoo. For example, in a lot of spells that involve candles, leaves and flowers are used. The same goes for spells that involve cleanses. For something more potent, the root is often employed. The state of the plant is also something to note. Some spells, such as love spells, require you to use fresh leaves or flowers while others call for dried leaves and flowers, which you find in cases that involve mojo bags.

Sometimes the leaves, roots, or stems are dried and then ground for use at the time and also for future purposes. So if the fresh herbs you acquired for your conjure are too much, you can dry up the excess and use them in a different conjure later. There are some cases where you are expected to ingest the conjure. This is mostly when the spell involves healing. You have to be careful in such cases because not a lot of research has been conducted to find out how our body interacts with all these plants. To stay on the safe side, avoid conjures that require you to ingest them without first talking to a specialist.

TYPES OF WORKINGS

The way you perform a conjure in Hoodoo is known as working. Each 'working' is carried out in a specific way. Sometimes, you work with wet ingredients and sometimes you work only with dry ingredients, but there are cases that call for both. Mojo bags, for example, are workings that require dry ingredients. Occasionally, you can add a little bit of oil to it, but oil is not considered wet. For a cleanse, more often than not the tools required are wet, which means fresh plants.

It's okay to alternate fresh plants with dry ones when you are carrying out your cleanses because all of them will be immersed in water. What you use doesn't significantly impact the outcome anyway. Below, we are going to learn about the different types of working I have mentioned. The recipes I share here are excellent templates to follow and if you do everything right, you can achieve the results you desire. You can also create your signature style by personalizing it, or adding a little bit of yourself into the work to make it uniquely suited for you.

My signature in any rootwork I do is the plants I use, because I harvest them from my small farm. Homegrown plants are not a requirement but I like to grow mine because I am intimately familiar with planting cycles according to the phases of the moon and how they can influence the energy in a plant. As I mentioned earlier, all plants have energy, and if you can cultivate these plants according to their cycles, you might be able to pick them for use when the energy is significantly higher. This is why even when you buy roots and herbs from other people, you should make sure they are from Hoodoo practitioners who know what they are doing. Their plants tend to be more powerful than regular ones. If you're interested in following up on this concept, I created a detailed plant manual in one of the books in my Hoodoo for Beginners series. But the point is, the more you practice your rootwork, the more adept you will be at it. Your adeptness will help you figure out some of the little nuances that add your signature to the recipe. For now, let's look at the different types of workings.

Spiritual Baths

Spiritual baths are cleanses for the body. A spiritual bath can cleanse you, your energy, and your aura. It can also serve as a tool through which you manifest a protective layer over your body, thereby keeping you safe from harm. People who feel they have been cursed also take spiritual baths to break free from whatever has latched onto them. Then there's my personal favorite; spiritual baths that can be used to create an aura of attraction. This is perfect for attracting love, wealth, or favor into your life.

Floor Washes

Floor washes are cleanses carried out for buildings. This could be your house, apartment or place of business. You use a floor wash to cleanse a space, either for yourself or for someone else. Just like the spiritual baths, a floor wash can be done for protection and also for attraction. I have done floor washes that fortify the space of my intended client. Spaces that are fortified by floor washes cannot be pene-trated by evil spirits. There is a way to ensure that even people who wish to do you harm will not feel comfortable anywhere near the space. This comes in very handy, particularly if you intend to wage war on those who stand against you and also protect your peace at the same time.

Mojo Bags

The best way to describe a mojo bag is like having your own personal genie to carry around. You don't need to make a wish because the spell is already tied to a specific desire. Also, you don't need to renew it after every time it performs for you. However, mojo bags have a shelf life. You need to reactivate them from time to time. There is no consensus about how long a mojo bag remains powerful, but when you carry one with you consistently for a long time, you develop a sixth sense that allows you to detect when its potency is waning. For now, I can only offer an estimate, which is anywhere from three to six weeks, depending on the type of ingredients that were used and the intention of the spell. Some mojo bags are created to protect and some are supposed to attract. Whatever the intention is, a mojo bag is easy to carry around to ensure that you have access to whatever it is you desire.

Conjure Oils

Conjure oils are like fuel to a fire. They tend to amplify whatever it is you are trying to create. Let's say you are doing a spell for love. A few drops of conjure oil suited for what your expectations are will raise the potency of that working from 50 percent to 150 percent. Conjure oils work well with cleanses, mojo bags, and your good old-fashioned rootwork.

A shortcut I recommend to beginners is to buy conjure oils from well-known Hoodoo practitioners. You can do this for the long term or at least until you have a handle on your craft. In many cases, conjure oils are added to rootwork, but there are also times when the conjure oil is the rootwork itself. If you are going for a job interview, for example, dabbing a little attraction oil on the pressure points in your body can make you more attractive to your potential employer. The same effect can be achieved when you are going out on a date. Command oils dabbed on your lips can make the listener do exactly what you want them to do. That is how potent conjure oils are.

Rootwork

Rootwork is the traditional name for spells or conjures. Since you will be working with many plants and roots (hence the name), there's a lot of emphasis on having a good understanding of the various types of spells, as well as the spiritual significance of plants. As much as plants figure into the development of a conjure, they are not the only tool required to make it successful. You need to be clear on your intentions. The spells you create summon spirits, but it is your intention that helps direct the spirit on what to do. If your intentions are not clear, the spirit can only do so much.

The timing of the day can also matter. Some rootwork needs to be carried out at night and some during the day, though of course there are spells that can be performed regardless of the time of the day. The duration of a spell also matters. These details are included in the recipes I will share with you in this book so you know how long you should allow a conjure to cook. This time allows the tools you use in it to release their energy into the conjure. Finally, the disposal of the tools after you are done with them also matters. I will talk about this aspect in more detail later on.

Now that we have familiarized ourselves with some of the basic concepts in Hoodoo, the next step is to look into the two main subjects of focus for this book, namely war and peace. I will explain why I chose this title and what I hope to achieve with it. It is provocative, but the explanation is simple and clear. Remember what I said about knowledge and how it helps you build a foundation for whatever spell you want to work on? Since you are obviously interested in spells relating to war and peace, it's important that you understand my intentions. This will ensure that your mind and the intentions that come from it are aligned with the objective of the spells I will share with you.

2

When the ancestors of African Americans first set foot on this land, they did so in bondage. Whatever life they had before they came was to be forgotten. But this didn't mean that they didn't have a community. In this community, they tried as much as possible to settle disputes amicably. But what happened when their dispute was against outsiders and the battle was unfairly stacked against them? How did my forefathers find a measure of justice when society had built a justice system meant to deny them that? They turned to Hoodoo for help. More than a century later, the system has been overturned and transformed into one that is more equitable and inclusive, but the battle for justice and fairness rages on.

In Chapter One, I talked about how life is balanced because we have good and bad on a scale together. It is impossible to go through life without experiencing both. Most of us know that it goes against the laws of nature to have a life filled with so much good that there is not a single tragedy or sad moment in it. Of course, we can't ignore the fact that these labels of good and bad mean different things to different people, so the burden of interpretation lies with each of us. I cannot tell you what success or a good life looks like for you. I cannot determine what grief, sadness, or pain means to you. But I am going to help you find a way to channel the emotions that these experiences might cause into something creative and empowering.

I am generally a very positive person, but my outlook on life is a little stoic, in that I never presume I have control over everything. Thankfully, my heritage has blessed me with a gift that ensures I am not completely helpless, no matter how hopeless a situation might seem. When life takes a dark turn -- and I am not referring only to tragedy, but to our day-to-day struggles with addiction, dysfunctional relationships, social injustice, and so on -- we need tools to help us come out on top. That is what the title of this chapter means. The goal is not to wage war on the rest of the world just to be declared the next dark king or queen. That is not my intention. My hope is that when you come to these dark times in your life, you have knowledge of the resources you can use to turn things around in your favor. Now let's focus on four critical aspects of war as they relate to Hoodoo practices.

CROSSING

When I hear the word cross, one of two things comes to mind. First, the cross on which Jesus was crucified, and second, the state of mind that every child fears their parent will become because of something they've done. Maybe this is just a black household thing, but if your mother or grandmother was cross with you, it meant you were in big trouble. Depending on the gravity of the offense, it could mean a slipper expertly thrown at your head, or harsh words poured deep into your soul. I usually prepared for the slipper to the head because my grandmother had a way with words that would have me thinking about my existence for weeks.

In Hoodoo, however, someone being cross with you is not an emotional state of mind. It is an action word; 'a crossing'. It means someone has taken offense to you and decided to act on their feelings. This offense might not be inspired by anything you have done but simply because you exist. Traditionally in Hoodoo, a crossing is a type of spell positioned on the path of the intended target so that when their foot crosses this path, the spell is triggered in their life.

A crossing in practical terms is a curse, and a curse in this context is not necessarily what Hollywood's depiction of black magic has shown us. It is usually intended to teach the target a lesson. Remember the client I talked about earlier who had been in an abusive relationship with someone who had no intention of letting go? Well, the spell I performed that drove him out of town like a bat out of hell was a crossing. I instructed her to put it on a footpath that she was certain he would take. There are other ways to implement this type of curse and I will share some of them when we get to the spells proper. But the general idea is that the foot of the target treads on the curse itself before it is activated.

In the old days, when a footpath was made of actual dirt, it was much easier to initiate a crossing. In modern times, though, conducting a crossing on asphalt and concrete requires a little bit of innovation or thinking outside the box. Crossings can be placed in the shoes of the intended target or mixed with dirt and spread across a path that you are sure they will follow. Certain precautions must be put in place, however, if you are going to do the latter, especially if that path leads to the front door of your house. Don't worry, these details will be ironed out in any spell I teach you that has to do with a crossing. For now, you merely need to understand what it means to cast a spell of this nature.

DIVINATION

My grandmother used to say "just because you know how to perform a spell does not mean you should do it." I pass that knowledge on to everyone who starts their Hoodoo journey through me. There are certain things you do in life that bring you to the point of no return. The moment you set yourself on that path, you activate a string of consequences that could have a negative impact on your life. If care is not taken, that singular decision to perform that spell might result in life-changing results that you did not anticipate… and I don't mean that in a good way. Most of the spells that you should not cast without thinking it through fall under the category of a crossing. This is my perspective on the subject and I believe my grandmother shared my feelings.

The question of casting a spell like a crossing is not about whether you are doing good or bad, but about karma. We know that some laws cannot be broken. These are natural laws that help to keep the scales balanced. If one side tips over, it will affect us all. When the motive behind your spell is to exact revenge on the target, apply caution. Don't just follow your emotions. Find out from your ancestors and the spirits that help ensure that your conjures are successful if this is something you should tamper with. They see things you cannot see. They are set on a path you cannot follow. This makes them wiser, especially when you consider that what you do might have a ripple effect that could come back to bite you.

Finding out if your ancestors approve requires divination. To divine the things of the spirit world is not as complicated as it sounds. You simply ask a question and wait for a yes or a no. It is that straightforward. The simplest way to divine is through a deck of cards. Shuffle it as best you can and concentrate your thoughts on the question, then when you're ready, ask. After asking, you simply turn over the card on top of the deck. If it is red, the answer is yes. If it is black, the answer is no. If you are skilled in the art of tarot reading, then you can try that too. However, for a beginner, a deck of cards is very simple and effective. Whatever response you get, respect and accept it. Give it seven days before trying again to see if their answers have changed. After all, it could simply be a question of timing.

JUSTIFICATION FOR WAR

The question of ethics when it comes to practicing Hoodoo is something I have received a lot of pushback on. Some people are curious about my opinions while others exhibit righteous indignation based on what they think should or shouldn't be done. I will simply share my opinions based on my many years of experience. The laws of the universe are not the same as the laws of humanity. The laws of humanity suggest things are black and white. There are a set of rules and you must obey them. The problem with that system is that some people are left out when it comes to justice. Race, social status, gender and even sexual orientation might put them at a disadvantage against their opponents. In such cases, would you say that the system is fair in addressing the problems of everyone?

The laws that guide the affairs of the universe, both on our physical plane and spiritual one, are quite different. Of course, there are still rules that should be obeyed. But in Hoodoo, the only enforcer is karma. The issue of right or wrong is treated on a case-by-case basis and the judge is not me or whomever helps you to set up a conjure. It is the person who is carrying out the spell. Hopefully, we all have an adequate understanding of what is right and wrong. Your conscience is there to keep you in check and it is your conscience that judges you. If you knowingly decide to do something wrong just so you can satisfy the spiteful spirit you have allowed to grow inside of you because of an offense you think someone has committed, that's on you.

You may find some of the spells shared here to be ethically compromising, but as I have tried to make clear, no spell is inherently good or bad. It is your intention alone that earns it that quality.

PERSONALIZING SPELLS

The final piece in this chapter explores the personal element in any conjure. A spell is made up of roots and herbs. The plant provides the energy that acts as a bridge that connects you with your ancestors. Your intention provides direction for the spell. However, personalizing the spells helps them successfully reach the intended target. To add a personal touch to a conjure is to link it directly to the target. You can do this in several ways.

Names

Our name is part of our identity and our identity is a strong part of who we are. So if someone attaches it to a conjure, we automatically become the intended target. There are many ways to use a person's name in a conjure. For example, you can carve it if you are working with candles, or you can write it on a piece of paper.

Body fluid

Blood, saliva, semen, vaginal discharge, urine, and sweat are examples of body fluids that can be used to personalize a spell. Body fluids when used in conjures are more potent because they create a stronger bond with the intended target. Body fluids are especially powerful in perfecting conjures that involve Hoodoo dolls.

Pictures

A picture is worth a thousand words. When it comes to doing a conjure, the picture of your target is a direct link to them. In the early days of photography, some people feared having their picture taken because they worried their spiritual essence would be captured in the image. I won't suggest this is true, but when you place a picture of your target in a spell, you bind them to it.

Personal belongings

We leave an imprint on items that belong to us. Items of sentimental value anchor us to memories attached to them so that even when we exit this world, anyone in possession of one of these items can still feel connected to us. To work a conjure, items of sentimental value might not be terribly effective, but pieces of clothing they have worn are perfect.

Underwear and intimate items are highly recommended. Shoes and socks can also be used for crossings.

Body clippings

A Hoodoo doll comes to life when you use body clippings such as nails and hair. Stitching the hair of the target on the head of the doll and stuffing the belly with nail clippings binds the doll to the target. Naming the doll completes the task. Burning body clippings when doing rootwork that involves candles is another way to use them.

Everything I have discussed so far forms the basis of your foundational knowledge of Hoodoo, though there is much more you need to learn. You can conduct additional research on the internet or look for a local Hoodoo practitioner to teach you the ropes. But you also need to practice. The point is that you need to keep learning so that you can keep growing. It is not just about the spells. Knowing the recipe and having the ingredients, as well as the know-how to carry out the conjure is just a fragment of your journey. As you continue to practice Hoodoo, you will develop intuitive abilities that help make you more effective. This skill can only be acquired through practice. Now that we have covered Hoodoo for war, let us look at Hoodoo for peace.

3

Rootwork for peace is more about protection than anything else. When we're young, our parents have the primary responsibility of protecting us. I was the 'apple of my parents' eye' and they did everything to keep me in a bubble, protected from the chaos of life. But as I grew, that bubble burst, and I was left to face the reality that the world can be a harsh place. Whether we're coping with everyday issues and problems or managing what can be turbulent relationships with those around us, whether we're reclusive or social butterflies, we can't escape the occasional socially awkward situation.

Learning to perform protection spells is not about creating a bubble that keeps you safe, but about silencing the voices of people who have made it their priority to harm your reputation. It is about setting up a barrier around yourself to keep out negative energy or bad vibes. It is about blocking access to you for people who might wish to do you harm. Protection is keeping you and everything you care about safe from anything and anyone who might have bad intentions.

One major area where we experience a lot of turbulence is in relationships. Regardless of the nature of these relationships, one common thread is that they are not perfect. We fight and argue and then try to make amends. But this does not always go smoothly. Our pride, our pain, and in some cases, our reluctance to see the other person's point of view become a threat to the success of that relationship. A Hoodoo spell of protection can help to put an end to these feuds and mend what has been broken. In this chapter, I want to expand your awareness of the types of protection available to you and explain why you need them.

THE NEED FOR PROTECTION

There is a direct relationship between peace and protection. When you are protected financially, physically, mentally, and emotionally, you have peace of mind. While life comes with its fair share of challenges, sometimes the biggest challenges come from people. Strangers, friends, foes, and even family will not always have your best interests at heart. No matter how amazing a person you are, evil will find a way to worm itself into your life. So your best defense is to diligently guard your peace and happiness. But that protection or peace that you are looking for will not be handed to you.

One of my favorite Bible quotes says, "...the kingdom of God suffers violence and the violent take it by force." Essentially, we live in a world filled with strife, so being a mild-mannered nice person will not always earn you your peace. You have to be bold and strong to claim it and I will give you five reasons to do so.

1. You need protection to thrive

A person whose life is plagued with troubles that rob them of their peace of mind cannot function at their best. Their ability to reach their full potential in life is compromised because they are in a constant struggle to survive. In some instances, your peace of mind may not be threatened by natural causes but by curses/crossings directed at you. One clear sign that you are being hunted lies with the types of dreams you have. If you are spiritually sensitive, your intuitive abilities will tell you what's happening. Much like when the hairs on the back of your neck rise, you just know something is off. Hoodoo conjures that are designed for protection will help to remove those things that threaten your survival. This will help your mind focus on other important things.

2. You need protection to keep a home

A contentious spouse or partner will nag you and look for opportunities to start fights. This is a recipe for disaster in any relationship. There are also other things that threaten the peace of a home. External forces such as in-laws or infidelity can damage your relationship. A little Hoodoo spell can ensure the faithfulness of your partner, tame harsh tongues, and even help your partner find a new reason to fall in love with you. Protection spells can avert a crisis and help you maintain a home where everyone feels safe and loved.

3. You need protection for positive energy

Negativity creates a dark pool of energy around a person, and anyone who comes in contact with them will almost immediately feel drained and exhausted. Some spirits are made from this dark energy, so anything they touch becomes corrupted. A chance encounter can cause you to cross paths with such spirits, and when that happens, your life can become a living hell. Even beyond this, latching on to negative energy might cause you to experience a long string of bad luck.

A Hoodoo conjure for protection will ensure that such dark entities have no access to you and have no chance to perpetuate any nefarious intention. A simple spiritual cleanse is an effective way to rid yourself of this problem. When it comes to people with negative energy, avoiding them completely works well too. But since that is not always possible, you can build a spiritual barrier around your home, office, business, body, and even the bodies of those you love.

4. You need protection to settle scores and obtain justice

Disputes can be settled in or outside of court. But sometimes, the process of helping you earn a favorable settlement can take time and many of us don't have time to wait. Perhaps people owe you money or creditors are breathing down your neck. A quick conjure can drive debtors to your doorstep with the money they owe you, which could buy you time with your creditors. And if you have a case in court that you feel is being manipulated to your detriment, you can turn the tide and claim victory, as many did during the slave trade era. Are you having drawn-out custody battles with an unreasonable ex? Hoodoo can provide you with a solution that shortens this process and initiates the kind of peace needed among all parties involved to bring about a happy ending.

5. You need protection to maintain good health

The gift of life and good health is something that people are rarely grateful for until it is taken away from them. When our minds are constantly troubled by stress, worry, and anxiety, our health can deteriorate. Too often, we prioritize our problems over our health. When the mind is in distress, the first place the impact is felt is in the body. Hoodoo might be a spiritual path, but it also has very strong physical impacts. Whenever you find yourself struggling, use a quick spell to unclog your mind, provide clarity, fire you up with inspiration, and most importantly, restore your peace. Trust me, your body will thank you.

TYPES OF PROTECTION

Protection spells are designed to service a variety of needs that we will get into later. However, these spells are presented in different packages. The knowledge of the types of protection available at this level will help you be more efficient at creating advanced spells as you grow in the craft. Protection spells are very tricky, especially when you are trying to reverse a curse or hold off the attack of a dark spirit. But mastering the basics will give you a great start.

1. Bodily protection

You are the center of your universe. If anything happens to you, your whole world crumbles. This is why you need to prioritize protective spells. Rootwork for body protection can be made in the form of a talisman or amulet. A talisman is designed to ward off evil eyes and makes you invisible to those seeking to do you harm. When my grandmother taught me this, she explained that it allows you to thrive right under the noses of your enemies.

There are also mojo bags made for protection. A protection mojo bag based on the intention can provide you or the person you created it for with physical protection, spiritual protection, or even both. You should have them on you everywhere you go. And finally, there are cleanses. If you suspect you have been cursed with a physical ailment, a cleanse is a great way to wash it off. The best part is that, unless it is specified otherwise, you can use a simple recipe for a cleanse to rid yourself of almost any curse that is manifesting as a physical ailment.

2. Protection for spaces

The most common protection conjure for spaces is a floor wash. The simplest method is to prepare the wash the same way you prepare a cleanse, and then wash the floor with it. The major difference is how you dispose of the leftover wash. We tend to dispose of the remnants of body cleanses in a stream or under running water. Washes, however, should be disposed of it under the dirt.

Speaking of dirt, because a space is anchored to the earth, you might be required to collect earth from specific places in order to include it in the preparation of a protection spell. Depending on what you need it for, you might need to collect dirt from a church, a police station, or a courthouse. In cases where you are dealing with nasty spirits, graveyard dirt might be required. The dirt might be used with other tools and either put in a jar or sprinkled across a doorway.

3. Travel protection

Travel is how some people earn a living, while many simply love doing it. But regardless of your means of travel, there are risks. A travel protection spell can help put your mind at ease and allow you to enjoy the journey rather than obsess over fears. Travel protection comes in very handy if you are going to places that may pose a threat to you. A mojo bag is best for a travel protection conjure, but you need to add an oil that attracts positive energy and spirits to you. This will ensure that no matter what happens, you will find favor every step of the way.

With that, we have come to the end of your foundation lessons on the art of rootwork in Hoodoo. In the next section, we will roll up our sleeves and get our hands dirty. Be patient. You may be anxious to resolve your situation or feel discontent because of self-doubt and low self-esteem, but your emotions must take a backseat. You need a clear mind, focused intentions, and above all, to believe in yourself. What you are about to do might seem impossible, but you have the knowledge and resources to do great things. And remember, you are not alone. Hoodoo is about putting the powers of your ancestors at your disposal. We will start with a spell for justice and war.

4

As ambitious as the subheading seems, the reality is less extreme. Even so, spells to get you justice and turn things in your favor should not be treated casually. The consequences of dabbling in something like this could have a significant ripple effect. Remember, karma is not something to mess with, because it will come back to haunt you.

I do understand, though, that waiting on the sidelines can be difficult, which is why I recommend the use of these spells, but only when you can't see any other way out. When you have exhausted every legal means to find justice but aren't making any progress, perhaps turning to help from the other side can give you the results you seek. While the hurt that others may cause us can make us feel an anger that needs to be pacified, we cannot use conjures every time someone does something that upsets us. As Gandhi said, "An eye for an eye makes the whole world blind."

Don't get me wrong - you deserve justice. Just don't make it a routine. But think of using Hoodoo as pressing the panic button. And now that we understand the gravity of utilizing Hoodoo, let's consider what should happen when you fight circumstances that seem bent on harming you. The first rule is to not allow yourself to be governed by your emotions. To have reached this point, chances are your emotions are all over the place. I understand this. But a good conjure requires focus. I am not saying that you should ignore what you feel, but make sure you are in charge of your emotions and not the other way around.

Second, do not allow yourself to be driven by the need to see the other person suffer. It is a long, treacherous ride if you choose to go down that path. Your focus should be on getting justice for yourself, nothing more. Frankly, there are people I wouldn't mind seeing suffer in this life, like an ex who mistreated me during our time together. We had a tumultuous breakup and I was strongly tempted to put a curse on him because he stole from me. But instead of allowing that pain to consume me, I focused on getting him to return what he owed me, which he eventually did. That for me was justice enough, though to be honest, if I saw him today and he was bald and pot-bellied, I would smile happily. But that is karma's job (along with poor life choices on his part), not mine. When doing a conjure of this nature, focus on getting justice over anything else, no matter how tempting that something else might be.

25 Spells for Justice and War

The spells here range from simple spells to more complex ones. They cover cleanses, washes, conjure oils, mojo bags, and candle work. There are spells to bring your enemies to ruin and spells to stop people who are robbing you behind your back. We have spells to put a homewrecker in their place and spells to ensure that a cheating partner is physically unable to continue doing so. Got a neighbor who is making your life miserable? I have a spell that will get them evicted and out of your life. The list of spells here covers a myriad of troubles. One word of caution: don't let the names of the spells fool you. Most of them have a bit more bark than bite, but they are nevertheless guaranteed to help you achieve satisfactory results.

DOMINATION OIL

Domination oil is a very important tool for preparing conjures that demand the manipulation of someone's emotions. You can use it to trigger guilt, inspire love, initiate obsession and much more. You can also use it to curse someone, get revenge, or force a situation to shift in your favor by using coercion. There are a few different ways to make this oil but we are going to use the one my grandmother taught me when I was just starting my training. This particular domination oil can only be used on the person that this conjure is prepared for.

The major ingredient in any domination spell is calamus root. It is used in any controlling or domination type of conjure. It has an appealing sweet scent that compels your intended target when infused with the other ingredients we will use. Calamus root is also known as sweet flag, and the amount of control it allows you to exert over a person's will is mind-boggling. If done right, it can turn even the most powerful people into your personal minion.

You Will Need

- Calamus root
- Sweet almond oil
- Licorice
- A personal effect from the target (hair, nail clippings, body fluid, etc.)
- Jar or bottle for storage

The Work

1. Put the person's effect in a bottle. Make sure it sits at the bottom.
2. Crush calamus root and licorice and pour them into the bottle.
3. Recite Psalm 35, which is a plea for judgment, as you prep the ingredients.

4. Pour the oil on top and allow the bottle to sit under the light of a waning moon.

5. Shake the bottle on the third night and return to the moonlight.

6. It is ready to use on the third day but if you started on the night of a full moon, wait until seven days have passed for maximum potency.

This oil can be applied to your skin if you are meeting the target in an intimate setting. You can also dab it on your hands just before a handshake if the target is someone you are having a business meeting with. In addition to adding it to another conjure, you can also apply it to a doll replica of your target and use it to control them.

CURSE YOUR ENEMIES

Knowing exactly who your enemies are is a rare privilege. It is very common for them to operate in the shadows or under the guise of friendship, so they have access to you and can do more damaging work. From here, they can also ensure that retaliation is difficult for you. However, when their identity is revealed, all bets are off. When someone has made it their life's mission to torment you, returning the favor is only natural and this conjure is perfect for doing so.

Vinegar has a sour taste and smell. In a conjure, it can ensure the target can no longer taste or enjoy the good things in life. It condemns them to a life of misery. It does the opposite of what a sweetening jar is supposed to do. I love its deceptive simplicity. Easy to make but when it takes effect, the impact is devastating. On a more positive note, vinegar in a conjure can also be used to break addictions. But not in this one. This is a curse for your enemies.

You Will Need

- Vinegar
- Hot pepper
- Ashes
- Name paper
- Pieces of broken glass
- Jar

The Work

1. Write the name of the target on the paper nine times.
2. Place the name paper in the jar with the written side facing up.
3. Put the hot pepper, ashes, and pieces of broken glass into the jar.
4. Pour in the vinegar almost up to the brim.
5. Cover the jar tightly and shake it vigorously.
6. Take the jar to a dark place in your house that receives no light. Your work is done.

As you prep your ingredients, pour all your anger and malice into it. For maximum impact, you can bury the jar in a graveyard. My students often ask me what brand of vinegar to use for this recipe, but my answer is always the same: It doesn't matter what brand you use, the outcome will be the same. The cheap white vinegar will do a fine job. You should focus on finding a high-quality jar that has a tight lid. When you shut it, you want it to stay shut.

NAIL THEM DOWN

If you worry that your competition is getting ahead of you, a conjure like this one will stop them in their tracks. People may employ all kinds of dirty tricks to get one over on you. You have earned the right to even out the score and put yourself in the lead. This crossing is without malice or misery. However, it can frustrate those who are used to being on top or winning. This is why it is perfect for court cases.

The main tool for this conjure is nails. Nails have a very strong significance in Hoodoo. They are made of iron and their shape, particularly the square railroad types, represent durability, permanence, and the inability to bend. Rusty nails are preferred in rootwork. The older they are, the more potent. Old railroad spikes have a dark spiritual energy that makes them particularly suitable for crossings, curses, and banishing spells. They also work in protection spells.

You Will Need

- Rusty old nails
- Honey
- Name paper or personal effect

The Work

1. If you have hair or other intimate items, skip to step two. If using name paper, write the name of the intended target on the paper three times.
2. Completely cover the item (name paper or personal effect) with honey.
3. Under the cover of darkness, nail the honey-covered item into the ground next to an active anthill.
4. Let nature run its course and your work is done.

It is a simple conjure but by the time the sun rises, your conjure will have initiated a sequence of events that will hinder your target. It is a neat and effective trick. As long as the nail remains where you put it, the spell remains active. The day the nail comes out, the spell is broken, so keep that in mind.

HOT FOOT POWDER

This spell holds a place in my heart because of the first proper banishment case I handled for a client. Remember the conjure I prepared for my client with the abusive ex? Well, this is the conjure I prepared with the help of my grandmother. It is perfect for those who are just getting their feet wet in rootwork. Of course, you could buy a pack of ready-to-use hot foot powder at a good Hoodoo store, but where is the fun in that? Besides, the ingredients for this conjure are simple tools you can find in your kitchen... except for sulfur, which I want to talk about before we perform the conjure.

Sulfur has some cosmetic purposes and is used in the treatment of skin issues. In spiritual rituals, however, sulfur is a powerful neutralizing tool designed to render harmful energy useless. When you create a conjure like this and intend to use it on someone, chances are they have hurt you greatly. Before you curse this person, the sulfur used in this conjure will ensure that what they have done to you is neutralized. Whether the harm they committed against you was a crossing, wickedness that came from their malicious heart or just pure negative energy, you need to use this to sever their hold on you as you send them away.

You Will Need

- Black pepper
- Habanero powder
- Cayenne pepper powder
- Black salt
- Charcoal powder
- Sulfur powder
- Red sandalwood powder

- Glass jar for storage
- Mixing bowl

The Work

1. Set your mixing bowl on your ancestral table with the tools assembled around it.
2. Pour the ingredients one at a time into the bowl. The order doesn't matter.
3. Meditate on your intentions and ensure that you are clear about what you want to achieve.
4. Mix the ingredients in the bowl.
5. When they are thoroughly mixed, pour the mixture into a glass container and seal it tightly.
6. Open it whenever you want to use it and pour its contents into the shoes of the target. Sprinkling it on a path they walk on is also effective.

This powder can be used again and again for multiple purposes. The ingredients (except for the sulfur) should be measured out equally and the quantity depends on how much you want to make. The sulfur should be measured one pinch to each tablespoon measurement of all the other ingredients. In other words, if you measure out one tablespoon of each ingredient, the sulfur should be one pinch. Increase this amount in direct proportion to the measurement I have provided here. This is important.

CONFUSION MIST

When people plot against you, there is reason to fear because there is strength in numbers. However, a little confusion in their midst can turn the tide in your favor. Ants band together but toss some ant powder on that bond and they will scatter and abandon their mission. This conjure works like ant powder, except it doesn't matter if it is a group of people or a single person plotting against you. The effect is the same. It will plant confusion in their hearts and cause them to falter in their plans for you.

The star of this conjure is the poppy seed. Opium is a mind-numbing drug and it is made from poppy seed. In rootwork, poppy seed numbs the mind and creates confusion. It can also be used in conjures for protection and for attracting luck. Poppy seed is excellent when you have court cases. Throw a little bit of confusion in the camp of your opponents and watch the team and their case against you fall to pieces and crumble from within. That is the beauty of this conjure. You don't need to do anything else other than the conjure. The confusion in the enemy camp will be triggered and you'll be able to swoop in and claim your victory.

You Will Need

- Poppy seeds
- Charcoal
- Personal effect of the target

- Incense burner

The Work

1. If you don't have a personal effect of the target, write their name on a piece of paper.
2. Light the charcoal.
3. Place the burning coal on the incense burner.
4. Toss the personal effects and poppy seeds into the incense burner.
5. As the smoke comes out, speak your intentions concisely and clearly to the smoke.
6. Wait until everything burns out completely and then toss the contents into a small hole in the ground and bury it.

For this conjure to work, your intention must be very clear. You cannot switch from one intention to another and you can only do one thing at a time. Smoke conjure can be very fickle, so it needs your strength and focus to direct it diligently. I suggest a cleanse like the one I shared with you in Chapter One. This will help you clear your mind. A little bit of meditation also helps to settle your emotions and iron out any confusion or doubts you may have. A scripture verse to calm you as you meditate might also be helpful.

SOUR LOVE LEMON SPELL

Marriage, and even relationships in general used to be between two people. But as with most things in today's world, that has changed. Sometimes it seems as though monogamy is a thing of the past. Even before I was born, relationships often involved a third party. My most common conjures related to relationships, in fact, are not about finding love but about getting my client's partner to give up a mistress or side dude.

I've seen men and women who have devoted themselves to their partners and, in many cases, helped in their partner's positive transformation, only to have someone else butt into their relationship and reap the rewards. This seems completely unfair and that is where a spell like this one comes in.

Lemons are bitter and sour but they are very medicinal, both for physical and spiritual purposes. They are used in simple conjures to sour things up for people and to throw some bitterness into the mix. The usual objective is to drive romantic couples apart. But these conjures can also be used to sour up business partnerships, dissolve friendships, and even break up marriages. If you have a third party plaguing your relationship and you suspect that things are becoming more serious, a quick souring spell would put a wedge between the love birds. A client couple who were under a souring curse felt like they could only see the worst in each other. This continued until they could no longer recognize who they were. In the end, they could barely stand the sight of each other. Thankfully, I was able to reverse it, but I'm telling you about it so you know what to expect.

You Will Need

- Paper
- Lemon
- Vinegar
- Hot pepper
- 9 pins

The Work

1. Write the full name of one half of the couple on the upper part of the paper.
2. Turn the paper upside down and clockwise and write down the full name of the other half.
3. Sprinkle a few drops of vinegar on the name paper and let it sit.
4. Cut the lemon in half.
5. Split the name paper down the middle.
6. Pour dried pepper flakes generously on one of the names and then place the other name on it.
7. Slowly lift both names and place them directly at the center of one half of the lemon.
8. Put the other half of the lemon on top and use the pins to hold the halves together.

9. Place the pinned-up lemon at the back of your
   freezer.

Keep your intentions clear as you prepare the conjure. You can add a little poppy seed to the conjure just to throw a little confusion into their situation. Keep the work there until what you want to happen has manifested. When it does, take out the lemon and bury it as is deep underground.

STOP A CRAZY BOSS

Most of us have had that crazy boss at one time in our careers who made our lives miserable. This person worked you to the bone but made you feel horrible every second you spent at the office. They pushed you past your limits and never gave you the credit you deserved for the work you put in. I had one of these in my younger years and I used this particular curse to ensure that they lost their job in the most painful way possible. Looking back, I don't feel bad about it. It was my revenge for everything I had been put through. If you have a boss like this, a conjure can help you get revenge, and it exacts it quickly.

The secret to the success of this conjure is a dead wasp. The sting of a wasp is not deadly but it can be very painful and cause someone to change course if they are in the path of this wasp. In Hoodoo conjures, the effects of a wasp work in a similar way. It is not fatal in any way but it hurts exactly where it is meant to. Put this in any crossing and you give that curse a sting. This particular conjure will ensure that the target loses their job in a painful way. Of course, I can't be the one to decide what pain means for your target. That is where your intention comes in. Think of how you want this to work. Be decisive. Do you want to hurt their career or just remove whatever favor they have with the company? Use that to anchor you as you prepare this simple but potent spell.

You Will Need

- A dead wasp
- Black thread
- Vinegar

The Work

1. Cut black thread about a foot long.
2. Soak the thread thoroughly in vinegar and leave it in there for about three minutes.
3. Pick up your dead wasp. Avoid the stinger as much as possible.
4. Tie the thread around the wasp three times. Keep it loose enough to prevent splitting the wasp but tight enough to keep it secure.
5. Tie the free end of the thread to the back of the door in your boss's office and your work is done.

If you are feeling extra petty, add some pepper to the vinegar when you soaked the thread. The sting, when the conjure is done, will be twice as painful. Here is a quick tip; hang your conjure somewhere where it's not too obvious. A dead wasp is one thing but seeing a dead wasp hanging on a thread is enough to spook even the staunchest non-believer. You don't want your target to know that someone is out to get them. It wouldn't change the outcome significantly, but they might suspect that their misfortune was the result of some spiritual assistance.

LOVE SPELL BREAKER

This is another common conjure that clients ask me to prepare for them. If you have never experienced what it is like to be cheated on by your partner with someone you know, be thankful. The pain from such an experience is unbearable. Can you imagine being betrayed by the one you love and then being forced to fight them?

I usually recommend communicating with your partner and then attempting to erase whatever hold the other person has on your partner. Beware, the third party in your relationship might resort to spells and other love-binding potions to keep your partner's attention, but if that's the case, this conjure will terminate that spell and give you a chance to reclaim your relationship.

For this conjure we'll work with two powerful roots; the High John root and the Jezebel root. Both play a strong role in spells that require dominance. Throwing your urine into the mix ensures that you are the one who has dominance. This way, not only are you removing the spell that has been cast over your loved one, but you are not leaving an empty space for someone else to occupy. You are asserting yourself as the dominant romantic figure in your partner's life. This can help prevent cheating in the future and if you perform other conjures along with this one, you can solidify your relationship and get the kind of justice you will not find in a courtroom.

You Will Need

- High John Root
- Jezebel root
- Lavender
- Cinnamon
- Your urine
- Transparent jar
- Picture of the target
- A tray

The Work

1. Pour your urine into a transparent jar.
2. Add the roots, lavender, and cinnamon into the urine.

3. Seal, shake vigorously, and set aside for eight days.
4. On the ninth day, place on a tray the photograph of the target who you suspect may be under a love spell. Pour the contents of the jar onto it.
5. Remove the picture and allow it to air dry before placing it on your altar.
6. Dispose of the spell by burying it.

Recite Psalm 37 as you perform this conjure. If you are preparing this for someone who is not your spouse/partner, swap out the urine with ammonia. And instead of putting the picture on your altar, bury it along with the contents of the spell. Don't forget to hold the jar away from your face when you open it on the ninth day. The smell can be quite overpowering!

ENEMY DUST

Enemy dust, or goofer dust, as it is more popularly known, is a conjure designed to bring harm to your enemies. The gravity of this rootwork tells you that this is not something you should do lightly. However, since this chapter is about getting justice, we can assume there is someone in your life who has declared themselves your mortal enemy. And in that case, you have every right to defend yourself, including by employing all the spiritual resources at your disposal. When my ancestors came to this land, they were subjected to impossible conditions and had no one to stand up for them.

It felt like everyone was against them, but this conjure gave them a fighting chance.

Graveyard dirt is a powerful tool to use in a conjure. You don't touch that stuff unless you mean business. It is possible to buy it from a Hoodoo store but the best way to obtain it is to go to the cemetery yourself and collect it. You must be very careful not to collect dirt from the grave of a person who was malicious in life, though, or you will have a malevolent spirit on your hands. It's best to collect dirt from the grave of someone related to you and whose life you have some basic knowledge of. But don't just collect the dirt; be sure to leave some kind of offering on the grave, like snacks, rum, or even flowers, as these are a few of the offerings favored by spirits.

You Will Need

- Graveyard dirt
- Charcoal
- Hot pepper (dried)
- Sulfur
- Iron filings
- Poppy seeds
- Storage jar

The Work

1. Blend the charcoal, pepper, sulfur, and poppy seeds separately until they turn to powder.
2. Put the blended ingredients together in a bowl and add graveyard dirt and iron filings.
3. Stir the mixture slowly counterclockwise 99 times.
4. Pour the contents into the storage jar and keep in the jar until you are ready to use.
5. To make your enemy sick, sprinkle some enemy dust in their shoes. Their legs will become swollen and develop sores.

Psalm 37 and Numbers 5:23 are scriptures you can recite as you stir the mix. There are many ways to use enemy dust, depending on the outcome you want. If you want your target to leave town and never return, sprinkle it on their path. If you want to destroy their marriage, put their names and that of their partner in a black bag filled with broken glass and enemy dust and then bury it at a crossroads. If you intend to bring long-term suffering, then refer to spell eleven.

LUCIFER'S DUST

In Christian mythology, Lucifer was one of the most beautiful angels. Because he was beloved and favored, he began to believe his beauty, talent, and angelic status entitled him to god-like devotion. This pride led to him being cast out of heaven. There are many like this among us, who possess an overinflated sense of self-importance. Their pride and narcissism cause them to treat people they consider beneath them in a deplorable way. Lucifer's dust will humble them and cause them to fall like Lucifer did.

You might think that with a name like this, you'd need the eye of a double-headed newt or something to make it happen. But the tools for this spell are simple kitchen ingredients that you have easy access to, like onions. This spell has the power to dissolve things that have an inherently dark nature. Things like debt, pride, and even curses can be melted down by onions. If your target is a prideful, narcissistic nightmare, the onions, along with the rest of the tools in this conjure will purge them of that spirit by serving them a healthy dose of humble pie. Think of this conjure as the needle that will deflate their ballooned egos. The outcome is always very satisfying.

You Will Need

- Onion powder
- Garlic powder
- Chili powder
- Granulated sugar (white)
- Doll

The Work

1. Make a slit in the doll representation of the target and set it aside.
2. Pour one tablespoon of sugar and onion powder into a clean mixing bowl.
3. Stir nine times clockwise.
4. Add one tablespoon of garlic powder to the mix and stir counterclockwise nine times.
5. Add one tablespoon of chili powder and seal the bowl.
6. Shake vigorously before setting down.
7. Empty contents of the bowl into the doll through the slit and sew it closed with nine stitches. Speak your intention clearly with each stitch.
8. Store the doll in a dark place until the conjure is no longer required.

Hoodoo dolls should be made for you by experts as per your requirements. The dolls are named and consecrated for your intended target. However, if you are making them yourself, the easiest way to do so is to use the personal effects of the target on the doll. The doll's hair should be made from the hair of your target. The fabric should be from clothes they have worn. Other personal effects like blood, nail clippings, and so on should be put in the belly of the doll. And finally, name the doll after the person it represents.

TORMENT YOUR ENEMY

There comes a time in your life when playing nice will only sink you deeper into a hole of despair. When that time comes, you have to be ready to take off your gloves, bare your fangs and let your enemy know that you are not someone to be trifled with. A conjure like this one is used to prolong the suffering of your enemy. If they are not backing down in their plot to ruin your life, there is no reason you should either. This is another conjure into which you can pour your malice and hatred. Naturally, I don't like the idea of hurting another person. But I also don't believe in being someone's doormat. If someone is stepping on you and you have talked to them and tried every reasonable means to stop them and they continue to be the source of your pain, it is perfectly acceptable to return the favor.

Candles are a very strong spiritual element in almost every faith. The use of candles during prayers and meditations is common. The light of a candle flame serves as a beacon in Hoodoo. It signals your ancestors and any spirits around, letting them know that their help is needed. Candles are also used as representational magic, which is what we will be doing in this conjure. There are figurine candles that you could use to represent the target, but for this spell, a regular candle will work fine. The color of the candle also plays a role in the conjure. A red candle is used in rootwork for passion or love workings. A yellow candle is used to enable you to focus and concentrate and it also creates an enhanced atmosphere of happiness. Black is used commonly for curses and that is exactly the kind of candle we will use here.

You Will Need

- Black candle
- Enemy dust
- Vinegar
- Cursing oil
- Name paper
- Jar
- Mixing bowl

The Work

1. Pour one cup of vinegar into a mixing bowl.
2. Dip the black candle into the vinegar, avoiding the wick completely.
3. Gently massage the cursing oil onto the candle as you hold it over the bowl of vinegar.
4. Set the candle down and light it. Perform the rest of this conjure under the light of this candle.
5. Write down the name of your target on the name paper three times.
6. Put the name paper into the jar and pour the vinegar over it.
7. Add the enemy dust and cursing oil into the jar and mix well.

8. Make your petition known as the candle burns. Be very clear and specific and repeat it as many times as needed until the candle burns out.
9. Seal the jar and take the candle scraps along with the cursed jar to bury at a very busy crossroads.

It doesn't matter how far away this enemy is from you. You will achieve the results you desire. And rest assured that this is a long-term thing. Your enemy will be trapped in a cycle of bad luck, misery, and suffering. The cursing oil used here is easy to prepare and I share the recipe in spell seventeen.

THE WITCH'S HAND

In the old days, people used to accuse female Hoodoo practitioners of being witches. That was their ignorance talking but we never bothered to correct them because, as much as they hated witches back then, they also feared them. The curse of a witch prevented many people from doing terrible things. This particular curse has nothing to do with a witch but we call it a witch's curse because a woman places it on a man. If you have a husband or partner who is abusive and just plain evil, and you feel that divorce is not an option, then you are in luck. A witch's curse is exactly what the doctor recommends in this instance.

The crow gets a bad rap in this world. Perhaps the color of its feathers and its piercing gaze make people uncomfortable, but they are wrong to associate it with evil just because of its appearance. In Hoodoo, crows bring good luck. When you see a crow on your path, you know good luck is coming to you. If you use the feathers of a crow in your conjure, you are simply summoning the magic of your ancestors. Crows are messengers from ancestral spirits and unless specifically stated otherwise, your ancestors often come bearing good-will messages. When you use crow feathers in a conjure like this one, you are amplifying the reach of your ancestors to make this curse more potent.

You Will Need

- Crow feathers
- Damiana
- Honey
- Almond oil
- Red clay soil
- White candle
- Mixing bowl
- Heat-resistant tray

The Work

1. Place a handful of crow feathers on a heat-resistant tray outside (for safety reasons).
2. Burn the feathers and wait until they turn to ash. Collect the ashes and move to your ancestral altar for the rest of the spell.
3. Light the white candle at your altar table.

4. In a bowl, mix the ashes, damiana, honey, almond oil, and red clay to form a thick paste.

5. Rub the paste on the palm of your hand. Let every inch be covered in it.

6. Kneel with your hands lifted and palms facing up and petition the spirits of your ancestors for help. Let them know the anguish you have suffered at the hands of this man.

7. Carry on until the clay is dry and then wash the conjure off without soap. It's best to do the wash outside so the spell goes straight to the soil. After this, your work is done.

At the end of the conjure, you will be imbued with the powers you need to dominate this evil man. The air of authority he has over you will diminish. You just need to be ready to rise to the occasion by asserting yourself. To maintain the power that this conjure gives you, renew it every six months. Some men are extremely stubborn in mind and spirit. To completely overpower them, you might need to renew it sooner or as soon as you notice the effects waning. Another option is to use the domination oil in place of the almond oil.

THE EVIL EYE BANISHER

There is a saying: Keep your friends close and your enemies closer. While it makes a lot of sense, you must understand that keeping your enemies close does not mean giving them access to you. The eye of the enemy is a curse, and it is constantly looking for what it can devour. Their access to you is one of the things that gives them power over you. But if they are unaware of what you are doing or of progress you are making in your life, they will not know where or how to attack you. A conjure like this blinds the eyes of wicked people and diminishes the power of their curse. Without access to you, their powers are useless. Use this spell to banish or diminish whatever means they have been using to monitor your movements.

This conjure is more like a daily cleanse than an actual spell. You may not know who your enemies are, as they like to operate from the shadows. They use the evil eye to send curses that fester and grow without your knowledge. A cleanse like this will reactivate every time you take a bath, making sure you do not fall victim to them. The main ingredient is salt. Salt is a powerful cleanse. It is more commonly used in protection spells than in spells for justice because it nullifies or renders spells useless. But for this purpose, we are using it to not only keep the evil eye out but to ensure that it does not affect you. If you are going to be casting spells of revenge and justice, a spell like this one ensures that you have the strength and invisibility required to stay powerful.

You Will Need

- Sea salt
- Bath soap
- Water

The Work

1. Sprinkle a tablespoon of sea salt into the water you wish to use to bathe.
2. Bless the soap you use on your skin.
3. Proceed to bathe as usual.
4. Perform the bathing ritual morning and night.
5. Drain the water from the tub as usual and allow your body to air dry.

If you have just performed a conjure seeking revenge or justice, wait until midnight of that same day to take this bath. If your spell is active (in the incubation time for the spell), you should carry out the salt cleanse every midnight until the conjure is set and then you can resume your normal routine. This is because spells can be physically and spiritually draining and you need to stay powered up. Understand that salt not only protects, it also rejuvenates. That is what we are using it for in this conjure.

END YOUR RELATIONSHIP

We've covered spells for ending relationships with outsiders. This one is for terminating your current relationship.

Sometimes, bringing a relationship to an end can be the most difficult decision you can ever make. You never know how your partner is going to take it. A spell like this will ensure that your relationship ends on a sweet note.

When creating conjures in Hoodoo, you focus on certain elements to create a desired result. You use a sweet tool for sweetening or a sour tool for souring. For this conjure, we are going to combine both elements so that we can ignite a breakup but still infuse some sweetness into it so that your partner, and yourself as well, don't suffer negative repercussions from that decision. While it is possible for exes to remain sweet towards each other, in most cases you need help from the other side to maintain the desired level of sweetness.

You Will Need

- Lemon peel
- Sugar (1 tbsp)
- Salt (1 tsp)
- 9 Brand new pins
- 3Licorice roots
- Name paper
- Jar

The Work

1. Write down your name and full birthday as well as that of your partner on the name paper three times.
2. On the other side of the paper, write down your intention, which in this case would be "gentle break up" nine times.
3. Fold the paper away from you and then speak your intentions over the paper before placing it in the jar.
4. Hold the licorice in your hands and summon every strength that you can. This is a command tool and by connecting it to your will, you dominate the spell. Put the licorice in the jar.
5. Next take a single pin and speak your intentions to it before adding it to the tools in the jar. Repeat the same process for the other eight pins.
6. For the salt, sugar, and lemon peel, put them individually in the jar but also ensure that you speak your intentions over them before you do so.
7. When you have put everything in, seal the jar tight and shake vigorously. Call out your name and that of your partner and demand the break-up.

Your tone as you call out your name and that of your partner should be commanding. This is not you making an request. Rather you are compelling the results you desire to manifest. Shake this jar as many times as possible throughout the day and store it in a dark but warm place. For extra potency, you can put a few drops of the domination oil you made earlier. The call-out and the shaking of the jar will continue until your relationship has come to a conclusive end. The moment it does, take the jar to your backyard and bury it there.

SILENCE YOUR ACCUSERS

Any rootwork you perform that involves the use of animal parts is going to be creepy by nature, and this is one of those. We don't delve into the creepy stuff because we want to, even though there are people who take pleasure in such things. This spell is used in cases where you have someone willing to testify or say something against you that could destroy your reputation, typically a witness in a court case. A conjure like this can silence that person and perhaps give you a fighting chance. Please note that this spell is not long-lasting. You are dealing with flesh, so as long as the meat remains, the spell will be active. Still, we know meat rots over time and so will the effect of the spell. So timing is important. Make sure you use it precisely when you need it.

Cow tongue is used in Hoodoo, Voodoo, and surprisingly, in ancient mystical arts as well. The tongue of a cow symbolizes the tongue of the target. When you nail that tongue down, the target is immobilized in their speech and will remain so until you either destroy the spell or nature takes its course. Here is a note of warning: the truth will always find its way out. So if what the other person is saying is the truth, this conjure will only give you temporary control over when it comes out. But if it is a lie, you have greater chances of subduing that person completely. There are forces you cannot mess with in life and the truth is one of them.

You Will Need

- Cow tongue
- Black thread and needle
- Domination oil
- Rusty nails
- Name paper
- Flat wood
- Preserving fluid and jar (optional)

The Work

1. Write the name of the target on the name paper nine times and set it aside.
2. Place the cow tongue on the wood and make a small incision in the center.
3. Fold the name paper away from you and insert it into the slit.
4. Soak the black thread in the domination oil for nine minutes and sew the incision shut with nine stitches.
5. Place the rusty nails nine points around the tongue to form a circle and nail the tongue down.
6. Command the tongue to be silent in matters against you and bury it far away from you as is.

7. If you need more time, put the tongue as it is into a
   jar big enough to hold it and pour the preserving
   fluid into the jar before sealing and burying it, as in
   step six.

You must bury this spell as soon as it is done. The tongue
must not see the light of day. Also, remember that this is a
temporary fix. There is some disagreement on exactly how
long this conjure lasts, but I would say you have from as little
as nine days to as much as three months, so time it carefully
and make the most of the time it buys you. But never forget
that if you are trying to silence the truth, you are fighting a
losing battle, because it will come out eventually.

ASHES TO ASHES CURSE

Ashes to ashes is a secret family recipe designed to bring
your enemies to their knees. I use this curse on people who
have made themselves a nuisance in my life. Perhaps due to
familial relationships, I cannot completely sever ties with
them. However, it doesn't mean that I have to put up with
their annoying behavior. A curse like this puts such people in
their place and makes them unable to negatively affect you in
any way, as they are too busy cleaning up the mess their lives
have become after this curse.

When you burn something, you generally reduce its significance to you, making it less likely to have any power over
you. You often turn the table of power in your favor and gain

dominance over something. In Hoodoo, we believe that the essence or spirit of a person/spirit can be found in the ashes of items attached to them. Say, for instance, your target's name is John. Burning a picture, cloth or name paper belonging to John will leave ashes in its wake. Those ashes carry the essence of John and because you are the one who burned the items, you gain dominance over John. So if John happens to be an enemy, you will have the power to crush him.

You Will Need

- Item linked to your target
- Mustard
- Sulfur
- Dry pepper
- Jar

The Work

1. The first step is to work on the item linked to your target. You have several options. You can burn their clothes, pictures, hair, or nail clippings. If you have none of these, you can carve their full names on a log of wood and burn it down to ashes.
2. Gather the ashes and put them in a jar.
3. Add mustard, pepper, and a pinch of sulfur to the ashes and mix thoroughly.

4. Seal the final product in the jar and store it in a dark place until you are ready to use it.

5. To use, just sprinkle a little bit of this powder across their path. I like to sneak a few drops of it onto their doormats.

Ashes to ashes puts a busybody in their place. It forces them to take their nose out of your business and put it back where it belongs; in their own business. The beauty of this curse (if there is such a thing) is that it wears off in a month or so. If they learn their lesson after the chaos you bring about, they can get their lives back. However, if they continue to be pesky and annoying, you can reach into that jar of reserves and toss a few drops their way again.

JOB LOSS CREATOR

Why would you want to cause anyone to lose their job? I had a client who, after nearly a decade in the industry, finally landed his dream job. The industry he was in is very competitive but that did not worry my client. It was the only place where he felt he could thrive in his natural element. His immediate supervisor, however, was a stumbling block to his success. For nearly three years, he tried to manage that relationship but things only seemed to get worse. His mental health deteriorated to the point where he was having nightmares. Leaving his job would mean giving up decades of work and his dreams as well, so the simplest solution was to cut off the thorn. And that is where this conjure came in handy.

The work is easy. We will be working with the enemy/goofer dust that we created earlier, as well as salt. We are also going to work with ashes, which we used in the previous conjure. Basically, we're making three different conjures for this circumstance. The caustic nature of this spell means you don't want this in your face, so the salt helps to cancel out that blowback, making it safe to use malice in this conjure without compromising your safety. We will talk about this more in the next chapter when we talk about protection spells.

You Will Need

- Enemy dust (Spell Nine)
- Salt
- Ashes (Spell Sixteen)
- Address of the target's place of work
- Jar

The Work

1. Prepare the enemy dust according to the previous instructions if you don't have any on hand.
2. Prepare the ashes for your target according to the previous instructions.

3. Mix enemy dust, ashes, and salt and store in a jar until you are ready to use it.

4. Scatter the mix at the target's place of work. Places where they are likely to step would be perfect.

5. If there is any left over, dispose of it at a crossroads and rinse out the jar with salt and water so that it can be used in the future.

My client's story is a very compelling reason to perform this conjure. You don't need to fabricate a story to justify your need for this conjure. You might be worried about what other people think but I am certain you have a good reason and the only person who needs to be okay with your decision is you. Doubts have a way of tampering with the effectiveness of a good conjure. So if you have doubts, maybe you should let this one go. But if you are certain that this is the right path to take, then by all means, get out there and take your pound of flesh.

THE CURSE OF AHITHOPHEL

David was one of my grandmother's favorite people in the Bible. She saw him as a man who was after God's heart and as a result, he enjoyed a lot of favors from God. One story she told me frequently was that of Ahithophel. You see, David's son, Absalom, was planning to destroy his father and take over the kingdom, so he surrounded himself with powerful and wise people. One of the wisest was Ahitophel.

David knew that with the counsel of this wise man, Absalom would succeed. So what did he do? He prayed for the wisdom of Ahithophel to become foolishness to anyone who heard him, and that was exactly what happened.

This conjure will make those who plot against you develop Ahithophel's curse. They don't become stupid or have decreased function of their brain but it will feel as though their counsel is not trustworthy enough to be applied. When they share their ideas with their bosses, potential clients, and investors, those people will not listen to them because what they hear sounds foolish. It is a perfect way to punish someone who has underestimated you. There are many ingredients in this spell but I am going to talk about the mustard seed. Mustard generally is used for planting seeds of doubt through gossip, and because we want to afflict the target with the curse of Ahithophel, that is exactly how this is going to play out. Their credibility, in terms of knowledge, will be called into question because of gossip.

You Will Need

- Brown paper
- Domination oil (Spell One)
- Poppy seeds
- Mustard seeds
- Black pepper
- Black thread
- Water

The Work

1. Cut a square shape from the brown paper and write your target's name on it nine times.
2. Dress the name paper by putting several drops of domination oil on it.
3. Add half a teaspoon of poppy seeds, mustard seeds, and black peppers to a mortar and grind them together.
4. Cut about 30cm of thread and another thread twice as long. Dip it in domination oil.
5. Place the name paper with the name of your target facing up and pour the ground seeds on the center of the paper.
6. Fold the edges of the paper around the center and use the thread to tie the base so that it forms a head.
7. Twist the rest of the paper to form arms and a body so it looks like a weird paper doll.
8. Use the second piece of thread to tie the arms and the body.
9. Dunk the paper doll in water three times and say the target's name every time you bring it out of the water.
10. Put the doll in your freezer and leave it there until you are done.

The spell concentrates on the head of your target and because it is now in a freezer, their wisdom will be frozen. The poppy seed in the mixture will guarantee confusion and fog up their mind so they are not able to think clearly. When you feel your target has paid the price for whatever it is they did to you, you can remove the doll from the freezer and dispose of it with fire.

MAKE YOUR ENEMY FAT

Sometimes attacking your enemy where you are sure it hurts them most is the key to stopping them. Some people are very vain about the way they look. If something were to alter their appearance for the worse, their pride and ego would take a hit. This conjure is designed to make the target gain weight no matter what they do. I am not a malicious person by nature but I can tell you that there are one or two people in my life whose dramatic weight gain would give me joy. I think I already mentioned one of them. If this is something you desire, this conjure is perfect for you.

One of the tools for this conjure is cinnamon. You use cinnamon to draw things to yourself. If you want to attract money into your life, for example, you use the tools that are associated with money, and then you include cinnamon to ensure that you attract the spirit of money. If you want to bring love into your life, you use the necessary tools for love, and then you include a dash of cinnamon to ensure that you attract love into your life. For this conjure, we are trying to attract a gluttonous spirit that pushes the target to eat more than they normally would, exercise less, and slowly eat themselves into their new weight. It is sneaky and may be petty but the outcome is always satisfying.

You Will Need

- Cinnamon
- Hot pepper lollipop
- Vinegar
- Name paper or picture of the target
- Jar
- Black candle
- Domination oil

The Work

1. Put the picture of the target in a jar. If you don't have a picture, you can write the person's name three times on a paper and put that in the jar.
2. Add a cup of vinegar, one tablespoon of cinnamon, and a few hot lollipops into the jar.
3. Stir clockwise and seal.
4. Dress the candle in domination oil and place it on top of the jar.
5. Call the target name three times and make your petition known. Command them to lose control over their eating habits.
6. Let the candle burn out completely and then wrap the spells in a black bag and toss it away in the trash

or bury it if you prefer to keep them this way for a long time.

If you use cursing oil instead of the domination oil, your target will develop stomach troubles that will lead to their weight gain. The domination oil ensures total loss of control over their eating and exercise habits. To end this, you can perform a reversing spell with their consent or let the spell out of the bag.

SEND SOMEONE AWAY SPELL

The presence of some people in our lives is overrated. The fact that they were at one point near and dear does not mean that they remain that way forever. It is possible that you have both served your purpose in each other's lives. Prolonging such relationships can create a negative atmosphere that will slowly eat away at you. However, simply leaving them might not be convenient. In a situation like this, you can perform this conjure and they will receive a letter or offer that will take them far away from you. It will not harm them in any way but it will save you the stress of having them remain in your life.

This conjure calls for the use of a red, seven-day candle. Seven-day candles are meant to be used for seven days, as the name implies. It does not mean that you must use them this way, but if you have a conjure that is supposed to follow a seven-day ritual, then a candle like this is more useful instead of buying one candle for each day. The use of these candles depends on the color. Red is for love work or cursing, black is definitely for cursing and white is for clarity. For this work, you will not be keeping a seven-day vigil but the energy signature bound to this particular candle is essential for this spell.

You Will Need

- Seven-day candle (red)
- A pinch of ground hot chili
- A pinch of garlic powder
- A few tiny drops of camphor essential oil
- Carving tool

The Work

1. Use the carving tool (could be a small knife, pin, toothpick, etc.) to carve the name of your target on the candle.
2. Poke three holes at the top of the candle.
3. Put all three ingredients in each of the holes in this order: pepper, garlic powder, and essential oil.
4. Set the candle down and light it.
5. Make a clear petition. An example would be, "Leave me [insert target's name] and never return."
6. Repeat these words over and over until the candle completely burns out.

7. Wrap the burned-out candles in foil paper and toss them in your trash can.

A spell like this has no malicious intent. Perhaps you even have a soft spot in your heart for your target. But their continued presence is driving you crazy. Perform this conjure once and within seven days, they will have no choice but to leave you for good. The life they will be called to is neither good nor bad. But in any case, you won't have to deal with them anymore.

MAKE A CHEATER IMPOTENT

A cheating partner is a torture for anyone. Beyond the emotional damage, there is the risk and exposure to all sorts of STDs. If your partner can't seem to control his sexual appetite, this conjure will help guarantee that he is unable to perform. If you still intend to have sex with or make babies with this person, this is not the right conjure for you. But if you want to punish a cheater, you are in for a treat.

Hoodoo often uses representational magic, meaning the items you work with are meant to represent your target. In this conjure, you will be working with an item that is meant to represent a specific part of the target's anatomy. Some people like to work with eggplant. Some use potatoes. My grandmother once used a banana. I prefer to work with something that best resembles the person's offending tool. So before you do anything, picture the organ that has now become public property and go to the market to find a food item that looks like it. It could be a zucchini, a carrot, cucumber, etc. Once you've found it, assemble the other tools.

You Will Need

- A food item that represents target's anatomy (must be solid)
- Pepper (the hotter, the better)
- Vinegar
- Name paper
- Black thread
- Nine pins
- Domination oil

The Work

1. Write the target's name and their date of birth on the paper three times.
2. Make an incision on the food product you are working with and put the name paper inside.
3. Bruise the pepper a little to release its oil, fragrance, and heat, and squeeze it into the cut next to the name paper.
4. Make smaller cuts on the food item/tool and insert bits of bruised pepper into it.
5. Dip the thread in the domination oil and then use it to tie around the food item nine times. Say these

words as you do, "[Insert full name of the target] listen to me. Your penis is now a dead tool. As you have brought me pain with it, through it, you will now know pain."

6. Use one pin to hold down one end of the thread to the food and use another pin to do the same to the other end.

7. Stick the remaining seven pins into the food item and imagine the actual organ receiving searing pain as you do so.

8. Put the food in a jar in which it can be completely submerged and pour vinegar over it.

9. Bury the jar in the middle of a crossroads. Perform a cleanse when you get home and relax. Your work is done.

For extra malicious work, bury the jar in a graveyard or toss some rusty nails into the jar of vinegar before you bury it. Your target will feel a burning heat from within his penis as it withers away on the outside. The long-term effect of a conjure like this is that even when the curse is reversed, it may never again properly rise to the occasion... if you know what I mean.

SUBDUE A CONTROLLING PERSON

Some people need a taste of their own medicine before they can learn their lesson in life. I made this conjure recently for one half of a gay couple. His partner was controlling, abusive and manipulative. When the couple first met, my client was a happy real estate agent who, even though he wasn't wealthy, was more than able to take care of his needs and even contribute to the upkeep of a home. But his partner was insecure and self-obsessed. He demanded that my client quit his job, drop his "crazy" friends and devote all his time to their relationship. Being young and in love, my client did just that, but this did not stop the demands.

In the end, his partner dumped him for someone younger, so to get back at him, I made this conjure to take away his independence and make him weak in mind so he would become subject to the control of others. The not-so-secret ingredient for the success of this conjure is rum. Traditionally, rum is a favored offering of spirits. A conjure like this causes the target to let their guard down and loosen their inhibitions. With the help of the other tools in this spell, you will expose the scared little child within the target and exploit all their vulnerabilities. Their willpower will be compromised, and they will have no choice but to submit to the will of other people.

You Will Need

- Licorice root
- Black pepper
- Cloves
- Rum

- Corn silk
- Name paper
- Black thread
- Jar

The Work

1. Write the name of the target on a paper three times.
2. Place the corn silk in the paper and wrap it up.
3. Use the black thread to bind the name paper and make sure it is completely covered by the thread.
4. Put the bound name paper in the jar with black pepper, licorice, and cloves.
5. Pour rum over it and then cover the jar.
6. Shake it vigorously and store it in a dark place.
7. Repeat this every day until you are sure they have learned their lesson.

Please note that their newfound submission will not be to just one person but to everyone who gives them a command. They will be aware of their responses and despair at how helpless they feel to disobey or go against anyone. They will have the same ugly spirit they had before but will be powerless to stop themselves from being obedient.

BAD NEIGHBOR BANISHER

A good neighbor can make a world of difference in how you experience your home. Having good neighbors can help you feel safe, and when you are distressed, they can be an additional source of comfort to you. However, if you are unfortunate to have bad neighbors, your home can become the last place you want to be. A nosy neighbor can be very annoying, but they are rarely mean-spirited. A bad neighbor, on the other hand, is something that has to be dealt with decisively. This conjure will bring about their eviction or swift relocation.

Hot pepper can be a terrible nuisance in our waking life. A little smudge on the skin can create great discomfort and this is precisely why we use it in curses and crossings. It offers enough torment and discomfort to make the target run for their lives. While this particular conjure targets your neighbor, it can be used on anyone who you have access to that you want removed from your environment. People who torment you in any way deserve an equal measure of what they do to you. However, you need physical access to them.

You Will Need

- Hot peppers (the spicier the better)
- Cooking oil
- Three rusty nails

- Nose mask (the fumes from the preparation can cause you to choke)
- Fire-resistant container

The Work

1. Set half a cup of cooking oil on a fire for about one minute, letting it heat up nicely.
2. Bruise the peppers so their oils and fragrance are released.
3. Put the pepper and the nails into the oil.
4. Stir clockwise and recite Matthew 11:28. Visualize your target as the yoke that will be taken out of your life.
5. The fumes from the oil will be strong. Be sure not to expose yourself to them.
6. Set the oil down and allow it to cool.
7. Extract the nails and place them under the doormat of your neighbor.
8. Toss the oil and pepper mix at a busy crossroads.

For those who still don't know, a crossroad is formed when two roads intersect to form an X. It is a spiritual point where the worlds between the living and the dead collide. The disposal of the leftovers from most conjures can be done here, so the spirits can consume the part of the conjure that is potent, leaving behind the harmless bits. If you want to use this banishing spell on someone other than your neighbor, you have to get it to a place where you are certain their feet will step.

SPEED UP DIVORCE

Divorce is never easy. It is a deliberate decision to separate yourself from someone whom you once loved and believed you would spend the rest of your life with. But sometimes things just don't work out. As painful as this process is, some spouses make it even harder by being extra difficult in court. They make unreasonable demands and see the court process as a means to punish their ex's. If you are saddled with such a person, this conjure is for you.

The foundation for almost every marriage is love. Whether it was real or imagined, love once existed between the two people involved and there is always evidence of it. A love note, the ticket from a play or movie watched together, the invitation to the wedding ceremony... whatever it is, this item can be used as the basis to petition the spirits for a swift divorce proceeding. This conjure is much easier if you had a church wedding or if a minister of the church officiated the wedding. If not, you will have to retrieve dirt from a place that represents your faith to include in the work.

You Will Need

- A love letter or some other item that symbolizes the love you shared

- Dirt from a courthouse
- Dirt from a church (or any religious building that represents your faith)
- Jar

The Work

1. Burn the item representing your token of affection until it is nothing but ash.
2. Gather the ash and pour it into a jar.
3. Add dirt from the courthouse and dirt from your place of worship.
4. Shake it up and spread it at the entrance of the home you share.
5. Cleanse the jar for future use and your work is done.

If you are making this for another couple, you must pour the mix at the entrance of the home of that couple. A swift divorce proceeding will ensue. If the conjure is for you, keep in mind that you will not be able to slow down the divorce process if you change your mind later on.

MAD WOMAN POWDER

Out of all the conjures in my book series, this is the most malicious and the most dangerous. I always ask my readers to apply caution before performing these conjures, but for this one, I am asking you to be twice as cautious. Some of the herbs you will work with are dangerous to ingest, so make sure you don't prepare this anywhere close to where you prepare your food. Also, wear gloves before you touch them. Another note of warning: do not use this conjure lightly. As the name implies, it will drive your target mad. If they have a history of mental health issues, this might make their madness permanent.

Mandrake root is a key ingredient in this spell. It is a member of the poisonous nightshade family and is known for its potent hallucinogenic properties. If used properly, it can cause an enemy to see their worst nightmares in their waking life. My grandmother told me that a spell of this nature is designed to torment the target to the point where they can no longer distinguish their nightmares from their real life. The madness that ensues is not chemically induced. And even when it is reversed, the target might never fully recover.

You Will Need

- Gloves and mask
- Mandrake roots (dried)
- Nightshade seeds (dried)
- Henbane flowers (dried)
- Four tablespoons of coconut flour
- Enemy dust (Spell Nine)
- A recent picture of the target

The Work

1. Put on your gloves and wear a face mask. Avoid hovering directly over the herbs as you prep them so you don't accidentally inhale.
2. Put the dried herbs together in a mortar and pound until they become powdery.
3. Pour in the coconut powder and set aside.
4. Prepare enemy dust according to spell nine. If you already have it, skip to the next step.
5. Burn the picture of the target and collect the ashes.
6. Add the ashes and enemy dust to the mandrake mixture.
7. Put contents in a jar and store in a dark place until you are ready to use it.

To use the madwoman powder, spread it on the path of the target or put it directly in their shoes. Perform a cleanse before and after you perform this conjure. The herbs used here are not commonly found, and for good reason. But if you know a good Hoodoo store, you should be able to place an order. Remember, just because you know how to do something doesn't mean you should do it. These spells are about getting justice. If you choose to ruin someone's life out of spite, it will come back to you in spades, so be careful.

5

P eace is something we take for granted until we no longer have it. We are either not aware of the gift of peace or we assume that it will always be there so we focus on our other needs. We want to be loved. We want wealth. We want health and we want the good things in life. But we don't realize that without peace, those things will be like a feast of ashes. Everything on our plate will look beautiful but will taste like ash.

When you dabble in spirit work, you cannot be too careful. A protection spell will ensure that whatever conjure you perform does not leave trails that lead back to you. Negative spirits can ride on those trails and use them as a means to torment you. Not because you did anything wrong but because that's their nature. Hoodoo takes us outside our physical world and into a world beyond. Not much is known about this other world. The only thing you can do is to ensure that you and your loved ones are well protected.

Another element you need to protect yourself from is people who are looking for opportunities to hurt you spiritually. You are not the only one who is practicing Hoodoo. And apart from Hoodoo, there are other spiritual practices that are similar but quite malicious. You or your loved ones could be put under a curse at any given time. The things you love and hold dear to your heart might be a source of envy for someone else who might take measures to destroy your happiness. Learning the basic art of protection spells can help to protect your peace, your life, and secure your happiness.

25 Spells for Peace and Protection

The spells in this chapter are designed to protect your health, mind, body, home, and love. Some spells can be made from common kitchen ingredients. A few of them will have to be bought from professional Hoodoo practitioners. All the spells here are easy to perform. Most importantly, you need to maintain a calm state of mind when you prepare a protective spell. Set your emotions aside, and focus on your breathing. Meditate if that's your thing, or maybe focus on scriptures, which we are going to use a lot here. The state of your mind can influence the outcome of the conjure so it's crucial to have it under control.

PROTECTION FOR THE MIND

When the enemy wants to attack, the first place they focus their resources on is your mind. Before they do anything physically, they destabilize you mentally. And so, when you enter the world of Hoodoo, you need to prioritize the protection of your mind. If your mind is an impenetrable fortress, there is very little someone can do on the outside that would negatively impact your peace. Apart from that, you need a calm and stable mind to be able to effectively perform conjures.

A simple, common but very effective ingredient in a protection spell is basil. Basil can be used in its herb form, or you could use the essential oil. One of the reasons we turn to essential oils is for the preservation of the integrity of that spell. When you use herbs in their plant form, the conjures expire sooner. So if you want something you can rely on to last longer, use the oils. However, if you have no problem making your protection spells weekly, you can use the herbs in their natural form.

You Will Need

- Almond oil (5 tbsp)
- Angelica oil (1/2 tbsp)
- Bay leaf
- Basil oil (1/2 tbsp)
- Sage oil (1/2 tbsp)

- Storage bottle

The Work

1. Warm-up your base oil (almond oil) a little. Putting it over hot water works perfectly. You don't want it hot, just warm enough to help it bond.
2. Crush the bay leaf and put it in the base, as it is warm.
3. Add the basil oil and twirl a bit.
4. Next, add the angelica oil and the sage oil.
5. Allow to sit for 10 minutes on your ancestral altar before transferring it to the bottle you will store it in.
6. Set the bottle under the light of a waning moon to fire up the energy in the oils.
7. Let the mixture sit for a week before you use it.

This oil is meant to be applied topically and in small doses. Apply it on your temporal lobes when you feel like you are being attacked mentally or dab a little on the palms of your hands and rub together before you perform a conjure. To get the most out of it, make this conjure at the start of a waning moon. If you are having nightmares, this oil is perfect, especially if they are of the spiritual variety. Recite Psalm 3 over the oil.

ALTAR OIL

Every rootwork in Hoodoo requires the blessings of your ancestors. This altar oil is a variation of what people commonly call Abramelin oil. You use this to summon the spirits that help you empower the conjure. This particular variety is also made to be a protection spell so you don't accidentally summon the wrong kind of spirit that might mess up your conjure or decide to be mischievous. So after protecting your mind, the next place you want to protect is the altar from where the power will be seeping in.

We are making a type of barrier oil. The stars of this conjure are frankincense and myrrh. They have long historical roots in almost every religion and are known to have healing properties, not just physically but the type of healing that restores spiritually, which is what we need for the mind. We are going to be using essential oils in this conjure because it saves time from preparing our own oil. Plus, if you want to start from scratch, you may not have easy access to the base ingredients.

You Will Need

- Olive oil (10 tbsp)
- Cedar oil (1 tbsp)
- Frankincense (4 tbsp)
- Myrrh (2 tbsp)
- Dark storage bottle

The Work

1. Start with the base oil first. Then add frankincense, myrrh, and cedar oil, in that order.
2. Optionally, you can add cedar wood chips to bring an earthiness to the mix.
3. Pour the oil mixture into the dark bottle and seal tightly.

Use this oil on your altar every morning. Recite Psalm 23 and call on the spirits of your ancestors to walk you through your day. Thank them for the help they offered you previously. Make your petitions for the day known to them and lean into the sense of safety they provide you. This is a relationship of trust, so you have to reach out, not just with your petitions but with your emotions.

PROTECTION CLEANSE

In the previous chapter, I shared a protection cleanse mainly for conjures that have to do with heavy emotions, like getting revenge or ensuring that justice is served. That's because some of the herbs you will tamper with and the feelings you have to confront in that process will elicit some malicious emotions. A protective cleanse like the one I shared will protect you from that. This one, on the other hand, is meant to set up barriers so you are always in a safe space.

The key ingredient in this conjure is hyssop. It's great for its medicinal uses and healing properties, but in Hoodoo, the use of hyssop is inspired by its role in the Bible. From the Old Testament when it was used for purification and cleansing to the New Testament when it was used on Jesus when he was bruised and battered, you can see the importance of it. If you have had a traumatic day or performed a rather hectic conjure, using this cleanse will heal you spiritually and at the same time create a protective barrier to ensure that the after-effects don't come into play in your day-to-day life.

You Will Need

- Hyssop
- Apple cider vinegar (2 tbsp)
- Salt
- Cedarwood essential oil
- Coconut milk (1 cup)

The Work

1. Bundle the hyssop in small bundles and set in a pot of water to boil.
2. Add salt to your bathwater while the hyssop heats up.
3. Add in the coconut milk, the apple cider vinegar, and a few drops of cedarwood essential oil.

4. When the water with the hyssop boils, add it to what you already have in the tub.
5. Step into the tub when the temperature is right for you and completely immerse yourself.
6. Sit up and use the hyssop bunches to wipe down your body. Visualize the negativity leaving your body as you do so.
7. Step out of the tub and air dry. Strain the herbs from the tub and drain the rest. Dispose of the leftovers at a crossroads.

Recite Psalm 51:7 as you rub your body down with the hyssop. Visualization is key here to imagine whatever you feel is plaguing you leaving your body. If you are into crystals, putting amethyst crystals in the tub water can enhance the healing and protective ambiance for your conjure.

SELF-PROTECTION

The world can be a scary place and while your home might be the place you feel safest, it still doesn't guarantee your safety. There are measures you can put in place to keep you protected at home, but what happens when you're out? What do you do when you encounter someone who curses you with an evil eye? My grandmother always advised me to be proactive. Don't wait until something happens before protecting yourself from it. Building a barrier of protection around yourself makes it difficult for such things to affect you.

As I've discussed throughout, Christianity played a significant role in the formation of Hoodoo. As a result, it often includes the use of saints and biblical scriptures for protection. In Hoodoo, it is believed that the church or dirt from the church is a protective haven for everyone. The church is considered sacred ground that evil spirits and malicious intentions cannot penetrate. In this particular conjure, we will be using church dirt to manifest a wall of protection around you.

You Will Need

- Your picture
- Salt
- Silver coin
- Three clear nails
- Six smooth river stones
- Dirt from a church ground
- Black pouch

The Work

1. Fill the black pouch with salt.
2. Put your picture into the pouch and add the dirt from the church.

3. Add the nails to keep you anchored, silver coin for spiritual protection, and river stones to push back any tide of affliction, then seal the pouch.
4. Bury it in your backyard, or on church, mosque, or temple grounds.

If you are burying the pouch on church grounds, you can skip the church dirt. If you are not a Christian, you need dirt affiliated with your place of worship, whatever that may be. This is because prayers are performed there and this attracts protective beings and entities. Psalm 59 is perfect for this conjure.

PATH PROTECTION

You can see how easy it is to step on a curse. Anyone can prepare spells that can be tossed on your path to create chaos in your life and all you have to do is to step on it for their intentions to be activated. If you suspect you have stepped on a curse, this simple conjure is a way to get rid of it before it sets in. It is most effective when you carry it out before the spell begins to manifest in your life. Of course, it's not always easy to know if you've stepped on something. You have to be spiritually intuitive and extra vigilant. Perhaps you saw something suspicious that looked like the remnants of a spell? In any case, acting swiftly will prevent further damage.

Onion has a way of drawing something out. My grandmother used to hate it when I left half an onion out for later use because she believed that a half onion, when exposed, draws into itself whatever is in its environment. That is what we will rely on for this conjure. Once it is positioned in the right place, it will draw out any negative energy or residue a spell has left behind. You can do this as a protective measure every time you come home, since you can't be sure what you stepped on while you were out.

You Will Need

- Onion
- Hyssop cleanse (Spell Three)

The Work

1. Cut a nice medium-sized onion vertically in two.
2. Rub your right foot with one half and your left foot with the other half.
3. Put on a clean pair of socks when you are done and proceed to execute the steps in Spell Three.
4. Toss out the onion and the leftovers of the hyssop cleanse.

The common Bible verse for protection is Psalm 91. Recite this as you soak in the bathtub. Use the power of visualization to picture whatever negative energy or spell you might have stepped on leaving your body. You need to see it to enhance the potency of the conjure.

BLOCK BLACK MAGIC

Before we are attacked, we often receive signs, especially if we are spiritually intuitive. We all have guards who watch over us. Have you ever met someone new and barely talked to them but all your alarms went off anyway? Something was warning you about them. That is your intuitive process kicking in. When you are spiritually attuned, something similar happens. You experience a sense of urgency that demands you to take action. My grandmother told me that most of the time this is your spirit guide alerting you to the danger ahead, and this conjure can be the first of many steps to keep yourself protected.

In rootwork, a juniper is considered to be a power plant that offers strength and protection. Because of its strong spiritual energy, we often use it in rootwork that gives us courage, strengthens our willpower and in this case, blocks out black magic. We are going to enhance the power levels of this plant by inserting it into a mojo bag that we will carry with us everywhere we go. Think of it as your spiritual bodyguard.

You Will Need

- Nine juniper berries
- Salt
- Camphor essential oil
- Red felt bag
- Bowl

The Work

1. In a bowl, mix two tablespoons of salt with three drops of camphor essential oil.
2. Pour the mix into the red bag and add the nine juniper berries.
3. Seal the bag and leave it overnight on your ancestral altar.
4. By morning, it is set. Carry it on your person at all times. Feed it with a protection oil every nine days.

I recommend this conjure if you are traveling through some place where dark magic is practiced a lot. You may not be the direct target of those dark spells but you could easily be caught in the crossfire. This mojo bag protects you from black magic, be it deliberate or accidental. If your stay in this place is longer, you might need to work on a protection spell that lasts longer.

HOME CLEANSE

When you arrive at a new place, be it for business or work, you need to do what you can to make it your own. The first step is to clean it up. You can hire a cleaning crew to help out but you would still need to perform a spiritual cleanse to remove any negative energy and drive off spirits that might want to do you harm. A cleanse of this nature is simple. You just need Florida water.

Florida water is rumored to be made from the legendary and mythical fountain of youth. Of course, this tale was fabricated for marketing purposes. The part that is real, though, is the spiritual properties of this water. It heals, cleanses, and helps to amplify protection spells. Initially, rootworkers used just one recipe. But over time, we discovered that it can be adapted to suit each individual. This is thanks in large part to the increase in the production of a variety of essential oils. I will give you the base formula here and you can create a blend that matches your identity based on gender, personality, element, and so on.

You Will Need

- White Rum [or vodka if you prefer]
- Orange peel (from one orange)
- Lemon peel (from one lemon)
- Cinnamon stick
- Bergamot essential oil [10 drops]
- Clove essential oil [10 drops]
- Rosemary essential oil (or the sprigs if you prefer) [10 drops]
- Orris root [one teaspoon]
- Rose petals [one cup]
- Basil [a few leaves, either fresh or dry]
- Three of any of the following oils: lavender, vanilla, jasmine, ylang-ylang, sage, neroli) [five drops of each]
- Bowl

For home cleanse:

- A broom that has never been used before
- Water

The Work

1. For your work to be very effective, begin preparations on the night of a full moon. This means that you need to gather your tools the day before.
2. In a bowl, mix one cup of white rum/vodka, essential oils, rose petals, orris root, basil, cinnamon stick, lemon, and orange peels.
3. Stir clockwise nine times and allow to sit for nine minutes on your altar.
4. Transfer the mix into a jar and then seal tight.
5. Place the jar in your window at midnight. Choose somewhere that the moonlight touches and leave it there until the moment just before the sun rises.
6. Set it aside somewhere cool and dark. Leave it to sit for the next 29 days.
7. Strain the herbs from the jar if you want and toss them in a pool of running water or use them as is.
8. To use in a home cleanse, mix one part Florida water and three parts water.
9. Sprinkle the mixture on your windows, door frames, corners of the house, and the floor.

10. Use the new broom to sweep the entire house towards the entrance. Continue sweeping down to the path. Let the whole house/room air dry and you are done.

Florida water has multiple uses. You can feed your mojo bag with it, wear it as a cologne, or spray it on your doorway as a shield. I like to put some drops in a bowl of water and put them beside my bed when I am having trouble remembering my dreams. Buying Florida water from professionals can save you time and effort too.

CALL ON THE SAINTS

Every traditional Hoodoo worker believes in the power of the saints. Each saint has a designated role. Some help to bring love into your life, some help you to get justice when you have been unfairly treated. Because we are dealing with protection, we are going to focus on the patron saint of divine protection and deliverance, Saint Michael. In the Christian faith, Saint Michael is believed to be an archangel, a warrior who can be depended on in the fight for good.

My grandmother taught me that no matter how much we think we know about Hoodoo and the world that lies beyond our own, we are not invincible. There are spiritual battles that will bring us to our knees and make us fear for our life. In such times, your powers, knowledge, and herbs might feel worthless, but this is not the time to give in to despair. It is instead when you must call on the divine to come to your aid. And this protection prayer/conjure is one of many you can perform during such periods.

You Will Need

- Image of Saint Michael
- Red candle
- Coffee powder
- Petition paper

The Work

1. Set down the image of Saint Michael at the center of your altar.
2. Light a red candle in front of it.
3. Write down your petition and your name three times.
4. Sprinkle coffee powder on the paper and fold towards you.
5. Burn the paper in the candle flame and pray to the archangel as you do so.
6. Pray for guidance, protection, and spiritual aid as you watch the candle burn out.
7. Gather the ash and candle residue to bury in your backyard. Leave the image of the saint on your altar until that feeling of dread is completely gone.

When you have finished, donate to either the police, veterans, or firefighters. People who have officially served in this capacity are close to the heart of Saint Michael, since he is the patron saint of protection. Donating to them will put you in his good graces. You can also leave offerings at your altar daily.

TRAVEL PROTECTION

When you or someone you love are going on a long journey, whether by road, air, or sea, it is natural to worry about your own or their well-being. Accidents happen and sometimes cannot be avoided. However, some accidents are instigated by malicious spirits who simply wish to harm and there are things you can do to ensure that you or the person you love can reach their destination safely without any negative incidents. And even beyond malicious spirits, if many people are aware of the trip, there could be someone who wants to see the traveler reach a tragic end. This tool can prevent that from happening.

Mugwort, which is the main ingredient in this conjure, is often used for astral travel. When you are on the astral plane, there are spirits that want to keep you trapped there. Mugwort repels such spirits and keeps you safe. Even though accidents happen, there are elements of spiritual attacks in certain accidents, and using this conjure will help to keep the target protected from those spiritual elements so that their journey is smooth and safe. For an added layer of protection, it will invite friendly spirits associated with travel to ensure safety to the destination and even a safe return.

You Will Need

- Mugwort
- Personal effect or name paper
- Green thread

The Work

1. Place the mugwort on a table. Spread the leaves out like a fan.
2. Place your personal effects at the center of this fan. If you are performing this conjure for someone else and you don't have their personal effect, you can write their name down three times on a piece of paper.
3. Roll the plants around the personal effect or name paper in a way that it completely covers it. Tuck in any rough edges.
4. Use the green thread to secure the mugwort so it stays in place. Fasten the thread to the wrapping so that one end of the thread is left dangling.
5. Use the dangling end to tie to the belt you are wearing or the handbag you will be carrying. Another way to use this is to hang it somewhere close to your seat. Just make sure it is close to you throughout your trip.

Before you use the thread to wrap the plant, you could allow it to soak in protection oil for a while. This is optional. But if you have protection oil on hand, it will help by adding extra power to the spell. When you are back from your trip, you must dispose of it properly, either by burying it at a crossroads far from your home or wrapping it in tin foil and discarding it in your trash can.

BONE POWDER

Despite what the name implies, bone powder is not made from any bone, whether human or animal. It is made from crushed rocks. We will be using three varieties here. The objective is to protect every conjure you make from eyes that might reveal your secret. My ancestors believed that the best fruit on a tree can attain its ripeness and beauty when it is hidden from everyone else. In the same way, your spell is potent and strongest when no one is aware of it. This is one of the reasons we bury our conjures when we've finished making them or hide them in a place no one can see.

Dirt and rock in Hoodoo hold strong spiritual properties. The things you find under the rock are also valuable but for this conjure, we are going to focus on the rock itself. In biblical times, certain grounds were considered hallowed because of the properties of the rock. Moses himself was asked to take off his shoes because the ground he stood on was holy. The rocks we work with here are not divine but they do possess the ability to erect spiritual barriers that will keep prying eyes out. The nature of the second requires a little bit of courage, as earth spells are not as malleable as those made from plants. Be strong.

You Will Need

- Mortar, dry and crushed
- Red brick dust
- Clay, dry and crushed
- Ashes obtained from burned cedar or pine tree wood
- Offerings for spirits
- Mixing bowl

The Work

1. Put all the crushed rocks into a mixing bowl.
2. Stir counterclockwise nine times. As you do so, make your petition known in clear and concise language. What you want to communicate is that the powder you make from this conjure will form an impenetrable ring of protection whenever you cast a circle and no one can enter that circle without your permission. Be very clear and deliberate about saying no one.
3. When you are done with your petition, put the contents of the mixing bowl into a jar and seal it shut.
4. Go to a graveyard or cemetery with the jar and offerings for the spirits.

5. Place the jar in front of the cemetery and speak to the spirits guarding it. Let them know that you have come with a petition and that you would like those who guard the place to answer your petition. Leave the jar and the offerings there for three nights.

6. The morning after the third night, pick up your jar and take it home. Whenever you want to prepare a conjure, use the dust from the jar to form a circle and perform the conjure within that circle. Nothing will be able to see or sense what you are doing within that circle.

Be very cautious about the type of cemetery you go to. Avoid abandoned and unkempt cemeteries, as angry spirits tend to roam such places. They might answer your petition but it will come at a cost that you might not even be aware of or be ready to pay. If you have ancestors at a particular cemetery, that would work best. But you have to make it a habit to visit the cemetery with offerings from time to time. Don't go there only when you need their help.

CLEAR EYES POWDER

There sometimes comes a point in our lives when we are confused. We look for answers but aren't able to find them because our mind is clouded with doubt, regrets, and other emotions that act as shackles. To break free, we perform conjures that will open our minds to the truth around us and keep us internally balanced. This is probably why when enemies attack, they flood our minds with doubts. The second you start questioning yourself, that will be the moment your defenses will become shaky and eventually fall apart … unless you fix it. That is what this conjure is for.

Sage is a cleanse that is used in Hoodoo, Voodoo, and even witchcraft. Its spiritual properties are highly revered, but people have overused it to the point where it has become a cliché. But don't doubt its strength. In this conjure, we are going to use sage along with other herbs to open up your mind and set you free from the lies that keep you bound and unable to fulfill your potential. Use it to rid yourself of fear so you can stand strong and defend yourself. No matter what the enemy throws at you, a clear mind can intuitively intercept attacks and keep your heart, hearth, and body protected.

You Will Need

- Eucalyptus leaves [dry]
- Sage [dry]
- Lemon leaves [dry]
- Mint [dry]
- Cornflower petals [dry]
- Five drops of protection oil
- Blue candle
- Jar

The Work

1. Put one cup each of all the dry herbs in a blender and grind them to powder.
2. Empty the herbs into a jar and then bless it.
3. Mix two tablespoons of the herbs and five drops of the protection oil you made in Spell One. It should form a loose paste.
4. Rub the blue candle with the paste you have made.
5. Light it for one hour until it completely burns out. Concentrate on the flame of the candle and picture the fire burning away any sense of doubt that has been imprinted in your mind.
6. On the day the candle burns out, gather the remnants and dispose of them at the crossroads. Your mind will be free and clear.

The clear mind powder can be used in multiple ways. If you have an enemy who is masquerading as a friend, putting a pinch of this powder in your shoes before stepping out will reveal that person to you. They will be the one who notices your shoes or steps on them. If you are feeling confused and torn between multiple decisions, grab a handful of this powder with some cloves and toss it into an open fire. A clear path will be revealed to you. The jar of powder should be stored in a cool dark place for future use.

PROTECTION FROM INJUSTICE

The world might sometimes seem like a place where life is fair to all but the reality is far different. At some point, most of us experience injustice that has the potential to derail us from fulfilling our destiny. Fate plays a role in the hand that life deals us, but the beauty is that it creates a balance where you can reclaim control and decide your own fate. One way to do that is to protect yourself from injustice in the world. This is especially important if you live in an environment where discrimination is rampant and the concept of fairness is foreign.

Oregano is one of the key ingredients in this conjure. It is a common herb used for cooking, but its spiritual properties are highly coveted. In Ancient Greece, oregano was believed to have been favored by the goddess of love, Aphrodite. This is probably why they used it in rituals for young married couples. And when you think about it, what greater protective force is there in life than love. Oregano conjures attract spirits that will feel protective towards you. The rum and salt in this spell will create a likable energy around you that makes it difficult for people to treat you unfairly. When you are favored, negative biases go out the window and when that happens injustice toward you becomes a rarity.

You Will Need

- Name paper
- Oregano
- Rum
- Black feather
- Salt
- Cotton wool or linen and twine
- Jar

The Work

1. Write your name or the name of your target on the paper three times.
2. Fold it towards you and put it in a jar.
3. Add the oregano, half cup of rum, six black feathers, and a teaspoon of salt.
4. Stuff the top of the jar with a fist full of cotton wool. If you don't have that, spread a piece of linen over the jar and tie it around the top with the twine.
5. Leave the spell outside among shrubs or under a tree. Every time you or the target of the spell is accused of something, shake the jar. The spell will be activated.

You can also use this spell whenever you feel threatened. The effect is pretty much the same. Think of the jar shaking process as ringing the bell that summons your protectors. Feed the jar with good quality rum at every full moon. This is not a moon working but it charges the spell and gives it a power boost. When it runs completely dry, it is time to prepare a new one.

SEXUAL PROTECTION

Cheating, whether physical or emotional, has destroyed countless relationships. But it is not always the actual act of cheating that brings a relationship down. What often does it is when sex is used to manipulate the person already in a committed relationship into continuing with what was supposed to be a one-night stand. Some women use this to hold a man down, either by getting pregnant or by sexually manipulating him into a submissive position in which he does whatever she wants. This can also happen when a man tries to claim a woman as his and then manipulate her into leaving her committed relationship. A conjure like this protects the target from being in such a position.

To inspire passion, with you having total control, we will use licorice root. This root is popular in candy but in spiritual work ranging from Hoodoo to European mysticism, it plays a significant role in spells and conjures that have to do with lust. It is used to compel the targets and also to strengthen romantic relationships, both of which are perfect for what we hope to achieve with this spell. Licorice root has a very strong essence and because we are going to be using it with domination oil, we need something to balance it out, like hickory nuts, which embody strength but flexibility at the same time. This is a balanced conjure that will not over-whelm the willpower of your partner. However, it will make them open to suggestions that will protect them from becoming sexually manipulated by anyone else, even if that person is using magic.

You Will Need

- Licorice root
- Hawthorn thorns
- Hickory nuts
- Domination oil
- Purple mojo bag
- Mixing bowl

The Work

1. Put one tablespoon of all the herbs into a mixing bowl.
2. Add three drops of domination oil and stir the mix clockwise.
3. Put everything into the mojo bag and hang it somewhere over the bed where you and your partner sleep.
4. Tonight, to prepare the conjure, ensure that you and your partner make love under that bag.
5. When you've finished, store the bag in a dark place. Your work is done.

Making love under a mojo bag enhances fidelity. When you put the mojo bag under the bed you make love on, it enhances passion in a relationship that is lacking it. Fair warning, after this conjure, your partner is going to experience a significant boost to their libido. So, prepare yourself for raunchy activities around the house.

BLACK SALT

Building a protection spell around your home is as basic as it gets. You want to keep negative energy out while ensuring that your home is open to spirits that come with goodwill and good tidings. Witches in olden days used to simply cast circles with salt or special crystals to achieve that result. But in Hoodoo, we prefer to add depth to that salt. Before you start making conjures, one of the first things you should learn how to do is to make the space safe where those conjures are performed, not just for you but for the spirits that show up, as well as the inhabitants of the home. This protection spell enhances the ambiance of your home, making it conducive for performing conjures.

To make a good protection spell, you need look no further than salt. Salt is a powerful protection agent in any spell or conjure. It has neutralizing powers, especially when you combine it with ashes. If you pour salt and ash over a conjure, it's a bit like pouring water over the flames of a roaring fire. You might not be able to put it out completely but you tamper with the energy of that spell, significantly reducing its potency. To make this combination fully protective, you need to be intentional about the type of salt used and how you integrate the ingredients.

You Will Need

- Sea salt
- Black pepper
- Charcoal
- Wood ash
- Jar

The Work

1. Blend the black pepper with the charcoal until it has a powdery consistency.
2. Add salt and wood ash to the mix. Stir clockwise 13 times.
3. When it is thoroughly mixed, put it into a jar and set it aside for when you need it.

Using black salt is simple. You can put it on a building, on a person, or on an object. Whenever you want to use this black salt, add a little bit of protection oil and rub it on whoever you want to be protected. If you are Catholic and have participated in Ash Wednesday, then you understand how this works. The mark doesn't have to be on their forehead or in any visible place. Just having black salt on their body is enough to identify them to the spirits you summon as beings who need to be protected. The same thing can be done to property that you want to keep out of evil hands. If you are protecting a building, use the black salt to cast a circle around it. For this conjure, it is best to work with wood ash extracted from pinewood. If you don't have access to that, you can work with regular wood. Reciting Psalm 91 as you prepare this conjure gives it a boost.

PROTECTION AND POWER HAND

Whether we like it or not, the art of Hoodoo is not an exclusive club. There are millions of people practicing it and they do it for a variety of reasons. Some people prefer to focus on darker workings; the type that involve dangerous spirits. These types of workings create curses that can permanently destabilize a person's life. In the previous chapter, we touched on one or two areas that might feel dark. But those are very mild compared to what people can do with Hoodoo. You can't control the actions of other people and so in this case, the best mode of attack is a strong defense. And that is what this conjure is for; to protect you from dark magic.

The working for this conjure is very messy, as you will be using your urine or the urine of the target you want to work with. You need to use your hands to prepare the work and this might require touching that urine. If you are squeamish about that, you can substitute urine for the person's cologne or if the conjure is for you, your own cologne. I strongly recommend using urine though, as it adds a personal element that binds the conjure to the target. This is about protection against dark magic. Cologne can be infused with some other ingredient that might not interact well with the tools you use for this conjure and might have an undesirable effect on the spell. Urine brings a personal signature that makes it binding and therefore stronger.

You Will Need

- Name paper
- High John root
- Red cotton thread
- Urine
- Salt

The Work

1. Use your hand to cut out a square shape from brown craft paper the size of your palm.
2. Write down your name or the target name on the paper three times using a pencil or permanent marker.
3. Drench the name paper in about two tablespoons of urine (or cologne, if that's what you've chosen).
4. Measure half a teaspoon of salt and sprinkle it on the name paper.
5. Place the High John root at the center of the name paper and then wrap the paper around it until the root is completely covered.

6. Bind the paper wrapping with red thread to make sure the paper is secure and stays in place. Be careful not to pull too tight, as the paper is completely drenched in urine!

7. Place it under the sun to dry for three days. When it is dry, you or the target must carry it with you at all times.

As always, I like to dip the thread that I work with in a conjure oil that is suitable for my intention. For example, since this is a protection conjure, I will use the protection oil on the thread. Mind you, this is not mandatory but simply a personal preference. Using it gives me an extra layer of comfort in the knowledge that I am getting full protection. To keep the power of this conjure strong and effective around the clock, you need to feed this charm with Florida water every seven days or every Monday. The recipe I shared in Spell Seven would be perfect for this.

EGG CLEANSE

If you have been hit with a curse or you suspect that you have been hit with a curse, a quick way to fix that is with an egg cleanse. This practice is very common in Hoodoo. Voodoo practitioners also use this method. When you use an egg in a conjure like this one, two things happen. You can divine if you have been cursed and then you can cleanse yourself from the curse. The egg will remove any doubts you may have and also draw out whatever it is that has been placed in your body. You don't have to wait until you are manifesting the physical symptoms of the curse. The second you suspect it or have received signs that you might be cursed, you should take this action.

For this ritual, we are going to combine holy water with the egg cleanse. You can obtain holy water from a church or make your own. As a Christian, I prefer to use holy water from my church but I know that not all of us share the same faith, so you can make your own according to your belief. The primary ingredient in making holy water is salt. The water should be obtained from a natural source, while the salt should be sea salt. Bless the salt and the water using the scriptures and then combine them. People who practice Buddhism, Hinduism, and others have their own versions of holy water. Research that and create a version of their recipe that you are comfortable with.

You Will Need

- Egg
- Frankincense (incense)
- Holy water
- White candle
- Jar

The Work

1. First, light your candle and place it on your altar.
2. Concentrate on the candle flames and draw strength from them. Know that you are safe, regardless of what the enemy might have done to you.
3. Place an uncooked medium-sized egg at the center of the altar.
4. In a small bowl, pour out the holy water and then dip the egg into it three times.
5. Starting from the crown of your head, rub the egg in a downwards and outwards direction without actually touching your skin or any part of your body. If you can have someone else do this for you, that would be ideal. You can be standing or lying down for this. Just ensure that the egg sweeps every part of your body.
6. When you are done, place the egg gently inside a jar and seal it. Take this jar to a crossroads where you will smash the egg at midnight. Declare that whatever curse was placed on your body is now done and gone.

Check the color of the egg after you have smashed it. If it is clear, it means that there was nothing on you. But if it is spotty or colored, it means that your suspicions were right; there was indeed a curse but it has now been lifted. Go back home and perform the hyssop cleanse to ensure that you are thoroughly purified and protected inside and out. If the curse has started physically manifesting in your body as some kind of sickness when you are rubbing down your body with the egg, you can touch the egg to the affected part of your body. One more tip: if you are using the Bible as you prepare your conjures, recite Psalm 23 and Psalm 91 when you light the candle before doing anything else.

MIRROR HONEY

When you work in a company or at an established organization, your biggest asset is not the number of degrees you have or the references that vouch for you, it is the quality of your ideas. If you can consistently bring in great ideas that drive up sales and push the company closer to its goals, you become a valuable asset. Especially if you know how to stand up for yourself and play office politics. This probably explains why some people are willing to steal ideas so they can secure their place in their organization. If you have an idea and are worried that someone might claim it as their own, a conjure like this one will protect your idea and keep it yours until you are ready to share it.

One of the tools we are going to use in this conjure is honey. People think of honey as a sweet ingredient and therefore think it can only be used in sweetening spells or in things that have to do with romance. While this is true, there is an aggressive side to honey if you know how to combine it with the right ingredients. Many protection spells can be made using honey. The idea is to sweeten the spirit that you summon so they favor you more. And when you are favored by spirits, you automatically fall under their protection. In this case, we are not trying to protect you, but your idea.

You Will Need

- Honey
- Silver mica powder
- Clove essential oil
- Wood ash
- Mixing bowl
- Jar

The Work

1. For this conjure, it is very important to be clear about what you want. So before you even start, write down two important petitions. The first one should clearly state what you want, which is to protect your intention or idea from a specific person or group of people. The second one is to appeal to the spirits you summon to keep your secret for you.
2. In a mixing bowl, add one tbsp of silver mica powder, five tablespoons of honey, and 10 drops of clove essential oil.
3. Stir the mixture clockwise and recite your first petition. Do this 12 times.

4. Now, stir the mixture counter-clockwise and recite your second petition. Do this 12 times.
5. Repeat the last two steps until the mixture has achieved an even consistency.
6. Pour into a jar and store in a dark place until you are done with what you are protecting.

When you are ready to execute your idea, take out the jar and bury it in your backyard. Alternatively, you can go to a crossroads and empty the contents of the jar there. Pour water over it when you are done and cleanse the jar. Wash your hands thoroughly when you finish handling the spell. Silver mica is relatively safe but it doesn't hurt to be cautious. This conjure can also be used to protect a person. You just need to modify your petition so it includes the name of the person you want to protect.

ASH PROTECTION JAR

When someone you love is in grave danger and you have no one to rely on for their protection, this ash protection jar comes in very handy. I have already talked about how useful ash is in protection spells. This one is a variation of one of the many conjures for protection made from ashes. When you need to protect someone other than yourself and you have zero to little experience performing conjures, this is the one I recommend. It is difficult to mess up, easy to make, and very, very effective, no matter how great a threat is posed.

One of my clients was a young wife of a soldier who was on active duty in a place where his life was constantly in danger. This protection jar was one of the many things we did to ensure that he carried out his missions successfully and came home with very little damage to his mind and body. For this conjure, we are going to be focusing on ashes made from burnt oak wood. Oak is synonymous with strength. Its roots go deep and it has a strong spiritual essence that is recognized in various faiths. Oak is considered the protector of the forest, so taking ashes from wood cut out of this tree extends that protection to whomever you prepare it for.

You Will Need

- Pinewood
- Oakwood
- Elmwood
- Name paper
- Jar

The Work

1. Gather the woods needed for this conjure together.
2. Look for somewhere safe and light the wood. Try not to use any chemical accelerant to get the fire started.
3. Recite Psalm 91 repeatedly over the flames as you wait for it to burn out.

4. When the flames are out, separate the coal and gather the ashes.
5. Write the target's name three times on the name paper.
6. Sprinkle a little bit of protection oil on it before putting it in the jar.
7. Cover the name paper with the ashes you have collected and seal it.
8. If you own your property, bury the jar next to your house. If not, take it to a church and bury it there.

This is one of the few conjures you cannot prepare without reciting a Bible verse. This Bible verse in particular is a very important part of the preparation process. So if you are not a person of faith, you might have to try some of the other simple protection spells I have shared with you throughout this book. You could throw some herbs into the flames to enhance it. A little bit of cinnamon will speed up your conjure. Some bay leaves or nutmeg will add some luck. Just be creative with it. As I said, it is difficult to go wrong with this one.

GATEKEEPER POWDER

The Bible mentions building a hedge of protection around a person's habitation, or home. This hedge of protection is meant to keep out evil spirits or people with evil intentions. When you lay this conjure around your home or place of business, you automatically put up a wall that keeps all within safe from evil. After using Florida water to cleanse the interior, I use a conjure like this to secure the perimeter. Your building becomes a fortress and no evil can reach you within its walls. The best part is that you can source the tools for the conjure from around the house and it is super easy to perform.

Red brick dust, which is one of the tools in this conjure, has its roots in early Hoodoo practice in New Orleans. My grandmother told me the homes back then were made from red brick, which represented security, so when protection conjures were made, they used red brick from existing buildings. It has something to do with anchoring the spiritual barrier to the land. To get the most out of your conjure, use old red bricks. The older they are, the richer the history, and the richer the history, the stronger the barrier spell. Nothing unnatural that is evil will be able to pass through the barrier without your permission.

You Will Need

- Cedarwood
- Red brick dust
- Churchyard dirt
- Mixing bowl
- Storage jar

The Work

1. Burn the cedar wood in a safe place and collect the ash.
2. Put the ashes, churchyard dirt, and red brick dust in a mixing bowl. Stir clockwise nine times and counter-clockwise nine times. Repeat this 11 times.
3. When you are done, put the mixture into a jar.
4. To use, hold the jar upright as you pour a line around what you want to protect. Whether a space or an entire building, the line you draw must connect end to end, so either draw a circle or a square.

To increase the potency of the conjure, you can add iron filings to it. I didn't include this in the main recipe because these are not easily found around the home. But the recipe is fine without it. You just get something stronger when you include iron filings. Some people use this gatekeeper powder at their windows to keep bad spirits from entering the home. For practical reasons, I don't do this because a strong wind could blow that line in and cause a mess. A much more convenient way to use it is to sprinkle it around the space you want to protect and then sweep it out with a broom that has never been used before.

BLACK SWEEP

Old age is something we don't have a cure for. We can use the services of a beautician and a surgeon to slow down the aging process but the reality is we still get old. One of the things I hate the most about aging is memory. As we get older, our memory starts to embarrass us. I remember once when I was looking for my reading glasses only to find them perched on my nose. People who don't practice Hoodoo remind me of myself in that situation. The solution to their problem is right under their noses but because they don't know about it, they scramble around helplessly in search of it.

For example, did you know that a feather can be used to cleanse and provide protection in a home? With a handful of feathers, you can curse someone who is troubling you, cast out an evil presence or negative energy from your home, create a protection spell that is impenetrable or even cure a disease that is the manifestation of a spiritual attack. It is that simple and because we are focusing on protection spells, this conjure is going to teach you how to use black feathers to set up a protection perimeter around yourself or your home. Black feathers have always gotten a bad rap but in Hoodoo they have strong, positive spiritual properties.

You Will Need

- A fistful of black feathers
- Florida water

The Work

1. Mist the person, space, or object you want to protect with Florida water. When you are using it on a person, you don't need to dilute it. When you're using it in a space, the water needs to be one part Florida water to four parts regular water.
2. Assemble the feathers in an orderly way with the pointy end facing upwards.
3. Band the pointy ends of the feathers you have assembled so the result looks like a bouquet and then tie it with twine. Hold the shaft and use it to make a downward sweep if you are protecting a person. For the space or object you want to cleanse and protect, make an outward sweep towards the main entrance.

As simple as this spell is, you need to understand that your intentions matter. When you sweep, don't just do it without thinking. Focus on what you hope to achieve and concentrate on the outcome. One thing that helps me is to visualize myself living in the results of what I have done. This anchors your intention to this particular moment and stays with you until what you intend to happen has manifested.

DEVIL TRAP

When you have pests like snails invading your garden, using pesticides can damage or destroy the plants growing there. The most effective way to get rid of them could instead be a beer trap. This trap has beer in it, which attracts snails, but when they come to drink it, they drown. This conjure works in the same way. It is a barrier type of protection that attracts any evil spirits patrolling the borders of your territory with what they like and then traps them like the snails. Mind you, it doesn't call evil spirits to your domain but simply ensures that those that are circling too close to your protected zone do not have the chance to break the barrier.

Iron sand is actually less sand and more a variety of metals. It has a magnetic component that makes it appealing in spiritual work. It is believed to attract wealth and luck. Its main purpose in this conjure is to amplify the power of the spell. Trapping evil spirits requires a lot of spiritual power. Adding iron sand to the mix will give you the power boost you need. It will also aid in keeping luck on your side so your protection spell, in addition to this devil's trap, holds up against the attack of the enemy. Perform this conjure alongside the Gatekeeper spell we learned earlier.

You Will Need

- Iron sand
- Honey

- Holy water
- Urine
- Long-neck bottle
- A bowl

The Work

1. In a bowl, pour half a cup of holy water, half a cup of urine, and half a cup of iron sand.
2. Mix the ingredients by lifting the bowl and slowly but steadily moving it around. Be careful not to move too vigorously so the ingredients do not spill on you. This doesn't affect the conjure. It is just a precaution for those who might be squeamish about working with urine.
3. Slowly and gently empty the contents of the bowl into the long-neck bottle. If there are remnants of iron sand at the bottom of the bowl, pour back some of the liquid from the bottle into the bowl and then back into the bottle until it's all in the bottle.
4. When you have completed the last step, take a little honey and smear it around the mouth of the bottle.
5. Take the bottle to the back entrance of your house or building. Bury it up to the neck and leave it there.

You can leave the bottle buried there for up to one week. On the seventh day, seal the bottle and carry it to the crossroads. Face east and throw the bottle over your left shoulder towards the west, say the words "evil be gone," and walk away. Do not look back.

DREAM PROTECTION

One of the clear indications a person has been cursed are recurring nightmares. The kind that come every single night and leave the victim emotionally drained and broken down. These dreams are often echoes of what the enemy has done to you. But they also could be your subconscious warning you that you are in imminent danger. In some cases, they are a tool that the enemy uses to invade your mind with fear and make you more susceptible to their attacks.

A conjure like this one is not as labor-intensive as some of the other ones we've learned. It is very easy to put together and works perfectly in emergencies. All you need is a bunch of hyssops. I have talked about the protective properties of hyssop and we are going to use that to our advantage here. What you need to do is grab a bundle of hyssop and sprinkle it with holy water or Florida water, if you have either on hand. Do not use both. Place the hyssop under your mattress where you lay your head. You should be able to sleep that night without having a nightmare.

A conjure like this protects you from dream attacks and can be effective for up to a month before you need to replace it. While this conjure works powerfully in keeping your nightmares at bay, you have to remember that this does not fix the problem. It only protects your mind to give you a fighting chance. You will still need to perform other conjures to counteract the effect of the curse.

MIRROR WORK

Sometimes, the things we wrestle with are very physical and ordinary. But the damage they cause can take years to fix, if fixing it is even possible. One such battle is when your reputation or name is being tarnished by vicious gossip. Other forms of possible problems could be the reckless behavior of others. At one point in our lives, many of us have had that friend who seems to have a disregard for the law, but we like them because they seem courageous and make us feel like we're invincible. The problem with these kinds of friends is that their actions can have negative consequences for you in the long term. A conjure like this protects you from physical problems like these and even spiritual ones too.

The main tool we will work with in this conjure is a mirror. The reflective nature of mirrors show you your true self, and in rootwork, they are used to bounce back arrows that have been thrown at you. It is not exactly a 'return-to-sender' type of spell, but just as the surface of a mirror has depth that cannot be penetrated, in Hoodoo it provides you with a barrier that keeps you safe from attacks brought on by gossip or the actions of other people. It is another simple spell that can be modified as you grow in the practice of Hoodoo.

You Will Need

- Two pieces of a mirror
- A name paper
- Black thread
- Protection oil
- Piece of red clothing

The Work

1. Write your name or the name of the target on both sides of the paper three times.
2. Apply three drops of protection oil to the names on each side.
3. Place the name paper on the back of one of the mirrors. If any edges of the name paper show from the sides of the mirror, fold them inwards.
4. Place the backside of the second mirror on top of the name paper.
5. Use the black thread to bind the mirrors together. Ensure it is securely in place.
6. Wrap the conjure in a piece of red clothing and store it in a dark place. It will continue to work for a long time.

The protection oil adds a spiritual layer to the protection spell so you are not just protecting yourself from physical attacks but spiritual ones as well. Hiding the conjure in a dark place ensures that it is secret and no one knows where it is coming from. And wrapping it in a cloth guarantees that the conjure continues to work even though it is hidden. Every other week or so, apply three drops of protection oil to the thread and continue doing this until you feel you are out of danger.

FOUR THIEVES' VINEGAR

This is one of the few conjures I prepare for myself and for clients that does not have its roots in the Bible or in old Hoodoo practice. According to the stories my grandmother told me, the four thieves' vinegar became popular around the time of the bubonic plague. Four thieves were caught stealing things off the bodies of victims who had died of the plague. People noticed that the thieves didn't become sick, even though touching the bodies and interacting with the deceased's clothes should have infected them. When the thieves were caught, they bargained for their lives with the recipe for the four thieves' vinegar in exchange for their freedom, and that was how the rest of the world became blessed with this knowledge.

Vinegar, despite its sour acidic taste, is very useful in any home. It has its domestic uses, which can be for cleaning, stain removal, and emergency first aid treatment. When ingested, it can help to cure a range of illnesses, from tummy troubles to skin diseases. It is not meant to be a treatment plan but it can help you stay away from the hospital for a long time. In Hoodoo, the traditional type of vinegar used is white vinegar. But for this conjure, we are going to go with apple cider vinegar. It is more stable and less excitable but twice as strong for protection spells.

You Will Need

- Apple cider vinegar (1 cup)
- Garlic
- Sage (2 tbsp)
- Lavender (2 tbsp)
- Rue (2 tbsp)
- Mint (2 tbsp)
- Thyme (2 tbsp)
- Rosemary (2 tbsp)
- Wormwood (2 tbsp)
- Jar with a plastic cover
- Mixing bowl
- Sieve

The Work

1. In a mixing bowl, add the apple cider vinegar,dry sage, rosemary, mint, lavender, thyme, rue, and wormwood.
2. Stir clockwise nine times and then pour the ingredients into the jar. Close tight and leave in a dark place for three weeks.
3. On the last day of the third week, bring out the jar.

4. Strain the contents through a sieve.
5. Set the herbs aside for disposal at a crossroads.
6. Return the liquid to the jar.
7. Slice two garlic cloves and add to the liquid in the jar.
8. Seal and leave the garlic in the liquid for three additional days.
9. On the third day, strain one last time and return the liquid to the jar. Your four thieves' vinegar is ready.

To use the four thieves' vinegar, you can add a few teaspoons of it to your bathwater. Alternatively, if you are carrying out a cleanse, adding two tablespoons in whatever type of cleanse you are performing should suffice. This is believed to ward off diseases and provide spiritual protection. In this particular conjure, every herb, apart from the garlic, is dry. But if you are going to work with fresh herbs, you need to let them sit in the vinegar for six weeks as opposed to three weeks. You cannot mix dry and fresh together. If you want fresh herbs in the conjure, then everything must be fresh.

HEALTH PROTECTION

Health is wealth, they say. To protect your health is to protect your wealth. Hoodoo conjures are not designed to take the place of medicine in your life. If you are sick, it is important to go to a doctor and get the right medical treatment. However, we make conjures to ensure that our overall health is protected. It is like protecting a house. We don't need a Hoodoo practitioner to build the house for us. We go to the experts for that. But to provide protection that ensures nothing evil affects our house, we use conjures. So think of your health as a home that houses everything about who you are and this recipe I am about to share with you is the thing that ensures it stays safe from evil.

Hospital dirt is very tricky to use in conjures. Some people believe that a hospital is a place of sickness and that using the dirt from the hospital will only invite more sickness into your home. I disagree. A hospital is not where people go to die; it is where they go to find healing. Hospitals were built for this purpose. In any hospital, you find people who have actually dedicated a large portion of their lives to understanding the art of healing. This creates an essence in the building, and taking dirt from such a place will invite spirits that are inclined to help with healing. You only use hospital dirt in extreme cases, like if you are very sick and undergoing treatment. A conjure like this one will speed up the healing process.

You Will Need

- Protection oil
- Hospital dirt (one cup)
- Name paper

The Work

1. Write your name or the name of the target for whom you want to perform this healing conjure.
2. Apply seven drops of protection oil on the name paper.
3. Place their hair in the center of the paper and then fold it away from you.
4. Take this folded paper to a crossroads.
5. Make a hole in the middle of this crossroads about the length of your hand.
6. Sprinkle some hospital dirt at the base of the hole and then place the folded paper in it.
7. Pour the rest of the hospital dirt on top of the paper and then cover up the hole with the dirt you dug out of the crossroads.
8. When you are done, walk backward three paces and then turn in the direction you are supposed to go. Do not look back.

If I sense that the sickness has been spiritually manipulated, when I turn my back on the hole, I toss salt over my left shoulder before leaving. When you or the target gets home, you (or they) should take a healing bath. The cleanse I recommended earlier would be perfect for this. Please remember, this does not mean you should abandon any medical recommendations or treatment you are undergoing.

This spell merely helps to create an added layer of fortification that can help speed up your healing and prevent recurrences.

CONCLUSION

The practice of Hoodoo is 70 percent knowledge and 30 percent curiosity. What I've shared with you in this book has laid a solid foundation, but you still need to be curious about how the process works. Be excited about exploring the interactions between the different tools you use. Keep an open mind as you practice because you will receive messages from the spirits telling you what to do and what not to do. These instructions may serve you personally or might be helpful for those around you. It is only through an open mind that you can figure these things out.

I feel very fulfilled in sharing what I know about Hoodoo. This is knowledge that has been passed down to me and some of what I shared with you is from discoveries I've made throughout my life. However, there are some things you will have to learn on your own, like patience, for example. While some conjures deliver satisfying results overnight, some will take their sweet time. There are conjures that will deliver the desired outcome almost immediately, but the results are not visible. But as we all know, just because you can't see something doesn't mean it isn't there. Giving up because you can't see what you want will only set you back. This is why you need to remember patience.

This book is just one of three that I have written so far. I implore you to read the previous works. They contain spells for love, wealth, and general happiness. I believe you can create the life you want. Life will hand you some tough moments, but those moments do not have to be the thing that defines your entire life. You can take the resources that Hoodoo has placed at your disposal to turn your situation around and create more opportunities to succeed. My ancestors did it. They came here broken, battered, and dehumanized, but they didn't allow that to be their story or the story of the generations to follow them.

They reclaimed power for themselves and built a community for their children and the children that follow. It doesn't matter what you have done, where you come from, or what people have said about you. You may not find willing help among your peers but the world beyond can help you reach your goals and build the life you want. I am truly honored to have played a part in showing you the way. Honor yourself by honoring the gifts left for us by those early Hoodoo practitioners.

Printed in the USA
CPSIA information can be obtained
at www.ICGtesting.com
LVHW021754080224
771343LV00002B/61